22

Best-selling Monologues Series from Smith and Kraus Publishers

60 SECONDS TO SHINE SERIES

Volume II: 221 One-Minute Monologues for Women

Volume III: Original One-Minute Monologues by Glenn Alterman

Volume IV: 221 One-Minute Monologues from Literature

Volume V: 101 Original One-Minute Monologues for Women ages 18–25

Volume VI: 221 One-Minute Monologues from Classic Plays

THE ULTIMATE AUDITION BOOK SERIES

Volume I: 222 Monologues, 2 Minutes & Under

Volume II: 222 Monologues, 2 Minutes & Under from Literature

Volume IV: 222 Comedy Monologues, 2 Minutes & Under

THE AUDITION ARSENAL SERIES

Audition Arsenal for Women in Their 20s:
101 Character Monologues by Type, 2 Minutes & Under

Audition Arsenal for Men in Their 20s:
101 Character Monologues by Type, 2 Minutes & Under

Audition Arsenal for Women in Their 30s:
101 Character Monologues by Type, 2 Minutes & Under

Audition Arsenal for Men in Their 30s:
101 Character Monologues by Type, 2 Minutes & Under

60 SECONDS TO *Shine*

VOLUME 6

221 ONE-MINUTE MONOLOGUES FROM CLASSIC PLAYS

EDITED BY
JOHN CAPECCI AND
IRENE ZIEGLER ASTON

MONOLOGUE AUDITION SERIES

A Smith and Kraus Book

Published by Smith and Kraus, Inc.
177 Lyme Road, Hanover, NH 03755
www.SmithandKraus.com

First Edition: August 2009
6 5 4 3 2 1

Cover and text design by Julia Hill Gignoux
Manufactured in the United States of America

The Monologue Audition Series ISSN 1067-134X

Library of Congress Cataloguing-in-Publication Data
60 seconds to shine. Volume 6, 221 one-minute monologues from classic plays / edited by John Capecci and Irene Ziegler Aston. — 1st ed.
p. cm. — (Monologue audition series, ISSN 1067-134X)
ISBN-10 1-57525-599-5 ISBN-13 978-1-57525-599-6
1. Monologues. 2. Acting—Auditions. 3. Men—Drama. I. Title: Sixty seconds to shine. II. Title: 221 one-minute monologues from classic plays. III. Title: Two hundred and twenty-one one-minute monologues from classic plays. IV. Title: Two hundred twenty-one one-minute monologues from classic plays. V. Capecci, John. VI. Aston, Irene Ziegler, 1955– VII. Series.

PN2080.A1225 2009
808.82'45089286—dc22
Library of Congress Control Number: 2009933209

NOTE: These monologues are intended to be used for audition and class study; permission is not required to use the material for those purposes. However, if there is a paid performance of any of the monologues included in this book, please contact the publisher for permission information.

CONTENTS

FEMALE MONOLOGUES

MALE MONOLOGUES

FEMALE MONOLOGUES

Agamemnon

Aeschylus

Translated by Carl R. Mueller

30s–40s

Dramatic

In order to change the wind, Agamemnon has sacrificed his daughter to the gods. Now, standing over his dead body, his wife, Klytaimnestra, a blood-spattered fiend of vengeance, addresses the outraged men of the Chorus.

My, how pious we are,
so suddenly!
Judge and jury all in place.
Passing judgment.
Curses,
hatred,
condemnation,
exile!

Where were you then,
where were they,
these citizens,
when *this* man,
at Aulis,
raised the knife to his daughter's throat,
Iphigeneia,
his daughter and mine,
caring not an iota that this was his child —

she was no more to him than a goat
from a flock of thousands! —
this sacrificial creature torn from my womb,
and for what?
To charm away the cutting winds of Thrace
and make some sailors happy!

Why not have exiled *him*,
driven *him* from the land,
for his vicious, polluting act that soiled us all?
No, you never gave it even a *first* thought,
let alone a second.
But of me and my just actions
you are a cruel and exacting judge.

Aias

Sophokles

Translated by Carl R. Mueller and Anna Krajewska-Wieczorek

20s

Dramatic

Tekmessa, captive wife of Aias, begs him not to go to war in search of a glorious death.

On the day you die, and, dying, leave me helpless,
On that same day, be certain that I will be seized,
Along with your boy, and dragged with force by the Greeks
To a life of slavery.
One of my masters, then,
Will say with insolent tongue:
"What have we here?
Aias' woman?
Our mightiest warrior's whore?
Fallen from a life of privilege to this!"

It's what they'll say. My fate will drive me on,
But you and all your house will suffer disgrace.
[. . .]
What evils we will suffer, the two of us,
If you should die! You are all I have, Aias,
All I can look to. Your spear ravaged my country.
My mother and father are dead: another fate
Took them off to dwell in Death's dark kingdom.
What land could I call home if I lost you?
What fortune would be mine? You, Aias:

You are all I have: my safety; all my safety.
Yes, and think of me, too: even me.
No true man forgets happiness he once knew.
Love begets love. And failure to remember
Kindness is no longer to be a noble man.

Alkestis

Euripides

Translated by Carl R. Mueller

20s

Dramatic

Alkestis, on the eve of her death, begs her husband, Admetos, King of Pherai, to watch over her children.

But now, Admetos, I have a request to make. [. . .] I know you love these children, love them as much as I. So please, I beg of you, make our children the masters of this house. Don't marry again, don't put another woman over them, a woman who will treat them less nobly than I, and out of envy beat them. I beg of you, my dear, don't. A new wife always hates the children of a previous marriage, hates them with a viper's poison. A son will have a defender in his father. Oh but, my poor dear girl, how will you ever grow to proper womanhood? How will she treat you? Will she ruin your reputation with scandalous tales, destroying your chances of marriage? A marriage your mother will never see, never stand by you in childbirth, hold your hand, comfort you with her love. I won't be here for that. I have to die. Not tomorrow, not the day after. But now. This minute. A brief second and I'll be among the dead. Good-bye. Be happy. I wish you joy. Admetos, be proud; you had a good wife. Children, you can say of your mother that she was the best of mothers.

All Mistaken, or The Mad Couple

James Howard

18

Comic

Mirida enjoys toying with her suitors.

My humor
Is to love no man, but to have as many
Love me as they please, come cut or long tail.
'Tis a rare diversion, to see what several
Ways my flock of lovers have in being
Ridiculous. Some of them sigh so damnably
That 'tis as troublesome as a windy day.
There's two of them that make their love together,
By languishing eye-casts; one of them has
One eye bigger than the other, and looks like a tumbler;
And that eye's like a musket
Bullet, and I expect every minute when he
Will hit me with it, he aims so right at me.
My other lover looks asquint, and to
See him cast languishing eyes would make a
Woman with child miscarry. There is also
A very fat man, Master Pinguister, and
A very lean man that loves me. I tell the
Fat man I cannot marry him till he's
Leaner, and the lean man I cannot marry
Him till he's fat. So one of them purges
And runs heats every morning, to pull down
His sides, and th'other makes his tailor stuff
His clothes to make him show fatter. O, what
Pleasure do I take in fooling of mankind!

All Mistaken, or The Mad Couple

James Howard

18

Comic

Mirida tells her suitor she would prefer hanging to marriage.

Hold, sir, I forbid the banns. I'd
Rather hear a long sermon than
Hear a parson ask me: Mirida,
Will you have this man your
Wedded husband, to have and to hold,
From this day forward, for better for worse
In sickness or in health and so forth,
Ay, and perhaps after we have been
Married half a year, one's
Husband falls into a deep consumption,
And will not do one the favor to
Die neither, then we must be
Ever feeding him with caudles.
Oh, from a husband with consumption
Deliver me. And think how weary I should be
Of thee, Philidor, when once we were
Chain'd together: the very name of
Wife would be a vomit to me; then
Nothing but "Where's my wife? Call
My wife to dinner, call my wife to supper";
And then at night, "Come wife, will you
Go to bed?" [. . .] If you please, sir, never propose
Marrying to us, till both of us have
Committed such faults as are death

By the law; then, instead of
Hanging us, marry us.
And then you shall hear how
Earnestly we shall petition
Your highness to be hang'd rather than
Married.

Amphitryon

Heinrich von Kleist

Translated by Martin Greenberg

20s

Dramatic

Alcmene has been tricked by Zeus into thinking that the lusty god is, in fact, her husband. The lord of Olympus has prepared a series of misadventures for the real Amphitryon that will keep him away from the palace while Zeus seduces Alcmene. When the real Amphitryon finally returns to his home, Alcmene no longer recognizes him, and here demands that he leave.

Vile creature! Odious man!
You dare to call me so? Before my husband's
awe-commanding countenance, I am
not shielded from your mania? You monster!
Far more hideous to me than bloated
shapes that squat in fens! What harm did I
do you that you should creep up on me under
cover of a night engendered out of Hell
and dribble your disgusting venom on my wings?
What more than that I caught your eye, corrupted
creature, like a glowworm, in the silence?
Oh, finally it's clear to me the mad
delusion under which I labored. What I
needed was the brightness of the sun by which to see
the difference between the cringing figure
of a vulgar peasant and the heroic architecture
of these royal limbs, between the ox and stag.
A curse on senses that surrendered to so gross
a hoax, a breast that rang so falsely to the touch,

a soul so little worth as not to know
its own true love! Without a sentry to mount guard
on my heart and keep it blameless,
I'll hide myself away, I swear,
where nothing lives, on a mountain peak not even
visited by owls. Your odious
deceit's succeeded, go! My peace of soul
is snapped and broken now.

Andromache

Euripides

Translated by Carl R. Mueller

20s

Dramatic

Andromache boldly addresses Menelaos, who has threatened to kill Andromache's son in retaliation for Andromache's so-called crimes against his daughter, the jealous, spiteful Hermione.

Reputation, reputation! How many countless, worthless men have you inflated to positions of greatness! Can a man as petty as you really have stood at the head of Greece's troops and wrested Troy from the hands of Priam? And is it now this sorry specimen of a man who comes huffing and puffing so self-importantly at the childish complaints of his childish daughter, ready to do battle against a woman already defeated, a slave, no less?

I'd say you've fallen from your perch, Menelaos. I consider you not good enough to have conquered Troy, and Troy too good ever to have been conquered by you. A molehill of an offense shouldn't need a mountain of correction. And, if it's true we women are a plague of evil, then men could do better than to imitate us.

As for me, I will both willingly and without sanctuary stand trial for poisoning your daughter and causing the barrenness she claims. Your son-in-law will be my judge, for I owe him in damages as much as I owe you if I'm guilty of making him childless. I rest my case.

Andromache

Euripides
Translated by Carl R. Mueller

20s
Dramatic

Andromache boldly addresses Menelaos, who has threatened to kill Andromache's son in retaliation for Andromache's so-called crimes against his daughter, the jealous, spiteful Hermione.

What a dismal lottery you offer me, Menelaos. A lottery of lives. To win means wretchedness, to lose, disaster. Maker of mountains out of molehills, listen to me. You're killing me. Why? What city have I betrayed? What child of yours have I killed? Which house have I set afire? I was forced into my master's bed. By a bully. Why kill me instead of him, when he's to blame? You're throwing out the cause for the effect. It's backwards. Where's the sense? [. . .]

I saw Hektor mangled to death behind chariot wheels. I saw Troy piteously put to the torch. Dragged by the hair, I was loaded on an Argive ship and sent into monstrous slavery here in Phthia, where I was served up as a mock bride to Hektor's murderers. But why wail over the past when present agonies can be trusted to give full measure? I had this boy, this one son left me, the light of my life, and now they'll slaughter him. It's their pleasure. But no, I won't let him die, not if my life can prevent it. If he lives, there's hope for him; but not to die for my son is a disgrace I could never bear. (*She moves away from the altar.*) There. I've left the altar. I'm in your hands. Slaughter, murder, imprison, hang me, as you choose.

Andromache

Euripides

Translated by Carl R. Mueller

20s

Dramatic

Too late, the jealous, spiteful Hermione sees the error of her ways. But true to form, she takes no responsibility for her behavior.

Please, oh please, Orestes, take me away, I beg you in the name of Zeus Protector of Family, take me as far away as you can, or to my father's palace! [. . .] If my husband comes home from Apollo at Delphi and finds me here, he'll make me die a disgraceful death, or make me a slave to his whore who once was my slave.

You may ask how I came to commit these crimes, as some might call them. The answer is, the visits of bad women. They were my undoing. Puffing me up with foolish advice.

"How can you allow this vile piece of war baggage," they would say, "to rule your house, share your husband's bed? By Hera, goddess of marriage, if she were in my house, meddling with my marriage, enjoying my husband, she wouldn't be alive to tell it!"

That's what they said. And I listened to them. [. . .] [N]ever, never — and I say it again, again — should husbands, husbands with sense, allow wives to visit their own wife at home! [. . .]

We must guard our houses with bolt and bars. Let other women in and you let in nothing good, but loads of harm.

Antigone

Sophokles

Translated by Carl R. Mueller and Anna Krajewska-Wieczorekk

20s

Dramatic

Antigone, daughter of Oedipus and Iokaste, defies her uncle Kreon's order that the body of her dead brother is not to be buried. When she is brought before him, Antigone tells Kreon what she thinks of his law.

Your edict, Kreon,
For all its strength, is mortal and weak when measured
Against the laws of the gods, unwritten, unshakable,
Laws not meant for now, but for ever,
For no man knows their age; laws that no
Proud spirit of a man could make me break,
For one day I must answer to the gods.
I know that I will die. How could I not know?
Even without your edict.
And yet, if I die now, before my time,
How can that be a hardship?
How can one live, as I do, surrounded by evil,
And not greet Death as a friend?

My death isn't important;
And yet, to see my brother lie dead and unburied
Is an agony beyond words. But this is nothing.
If you think me foolish, Kreon, me and my acts,
Perhaps I'm judged a fool by another fool.

Arden of Feversham

Anonymous

20s

Dramatic

England. Arden's passionate young wife, Alice, has been having an affair with Mosbie, a man in her husband's employ. When Mosbie tries to end things, Alice erupts with great fire, revealing the depth of her obsession.

Is this the end of all thy solemn oaths?
Is this the fruit thy reconcilement buds?
Have I for this given thee so many favours,
Incurred my husband's hate, and, out alas!
Made shipwreck of mine honour for thy sake?
And dost thou say "henceforward know me not"?
Remember, when I lock'd thee in my closet,
What were thy words and mine; did we not both
Decree to murder Arden in the night?
The heavens can witness, and the world can tell,
Before I saw that falsehood look of thine,
'Fore I was tangled with thy 'ticing speech,
Arden to me was dearer than my soul, —
And shall be still: base peasant, get thee gone,
And boast not of thy conquest over me,
Gotten by witchcraft and mere sorcery!
For what hast thou to countenance my love,
Being descended of a noble house,
And matched already with a gentleman
Whose servant thou may'st be! — and so farewell.

Back from the Country

From the Villeggiatura Trilogy

Carlo Goldoni

Translated by Robert Cornthwaite

25–35

Comic

Giacinta reveals how she is able to push away thoughts of her lost love, Guglielmo. (Methinks she doth pusheth too much.)

Let's just say heaven is on my side. You know how upset I was? Well, I tried to distract myself by reading a book I found. It was a revelation! It's called "Home Remedies for Mental Disease, or What to Do When You Are Losing Your Mind." Among other things I learned from this wonderful book: "When you are troubled by negative thoughts, you must try to concentrate on the positive." It says here we are like a machine. We must laugh a lot to shake the machine and keep it going. Our brain is full of tiny little cells where thousands of different thoughts are locked up and ready to pop out. Will Power can open and close these tiny cells whenever it wants to, and Reason tells Will Power to close this one and open that one. For instance, when the little box in my brain makes me think of Guglielmo, I have to switch over to Reason; and Reason tells Will Power to open up other little boxes I have up there, containing Duty thoughts and Honesty and all that. If they don't pop right out, I can float around in neutral for awhile, thinking about Clothes and Card Games and the Lottery and Food and things like that. And if Reason won't work and Will Power gets stuck, I shake the whole machine. I jump up and clap my hands and laugh a lot until the machine starts going again and the tiny little evil boxes are all closed and Reason can open up the tiny little good ones — and then I have Will Power again!

The Bankrupt

George Henry Boker

20s

Dramatic

1853, London. Amy's husband, Edward, has run afoul of a plot to ruin him financially. His enemy's final coup is to trick Edward into thinking that Amy has been unfaithful. When Edward angrily demands that Amy leave their house, she tearfully begs him to allow her to stay, if only to be a mother to their children.

Edward, I beseech you to pardon me! I do not ask to be your wife again; I only beg to be allowed to remain near you — wait upon you — to toil for you — to be your slave. Lest you should think my humility beneath me, it is not for your sake, alone, I ask it. A mother's heart cries through my lowly prayer. What will our young and helpless children do when I am far away? Whose hand shall smooth their pillows; or allay our little sufferers' agonies when sickness withers them? Whose hand shall join their rosy palms in prayer to the great power whom we so much offend? And if Heaven's wisdom should remove them hence, as it has done with one before their time — the child we buried in the spring, my husband; among the violets and early flowers, dropped like a severed bud — oh! then, what hand would not desecrate the dead, if it performed those offices of love which Heaven has sanctified to me alone? Think of it well. I only ask to live beside my children. I promise you, I will not vex your thoughts, by keeping my poor person in your sight! [EDWARD: Your female eloquence is lost on me. I prepared myself for these tricks of the tongue.] [. . .] I am not weeping to make you pity me. I do not wish to soften you by any but rational means.

These tears are shed over the disgrace which is about to fall upon our children. You have no right to forget them in your passion. You have no right — Oh! Edward, if my heart breaks down, and I am so choked with sorrow, my silence does not prove my cause unjust. (*Weeps.*)

The Bear

Anton Chekhov

Translated by Carol Rocamora

30 -40

Comic

Popova has sworn to be faithful to her dead husband, even if he was not to her.

A man! (*With a malicious laugh.*) A man, faithful and true in love! Tell me about it! That's news to me! (*Passionately.*) What right have you to say that? A man, faithful and true in love! Now that we're on the subject, then let me inform you, for your information, that of all the men I've ever known or shall know, the noblest among them was my late husband . . . I loved him passionately, with all of my being, as only a young and progressive-minded woman can love; I gave him my youth, my happiness, my life, my fortune, I lived and breathed for him, I worshipped the ground he walked on, like a heathen . . . and what happened? This noblest of men has shamelessly betrayed me at every opportunity! After his death I found drawers full of love letters in his desk, and while he was alive — I shudder to remember it — he would leave me alone for weeks at a time, he would chase other woman right under my nose, he was unfaithful to me, he squandered my money, he laughed at my feelings . . . And in spite of it all, I loved him and remained true to him . . . And what's more, he died, and I still remain faithful and true to him. I've buried myself forever between these four walls, I shall wear these widow's weeds unto my grave . . .

The Beaux' Stratagem

George Farquhar

40+

Comic

Mrs. Sullen warns her sister-in-law of the pitfalls of marriage.

O Sister, Sister! if ever you marry, beware of a sullen, silent Sot, one that's always musing, but never thinks: — There's some Diversion in a talking Blockhead; and since a woman must wear Chains, I wou'd have the Pleasure of hearing 'em rattle a little. — Now you shall see, but take this by the way — He came home this Morning at his usual Hour of Four, waken'd me out of a sweet Dream of something else, by tumbling over the Tea-table, which he broke all to pieces, after his Man and he had rowl'd about the Room like sick Passengers in a Storm, he comes flounce into Bed, dead as a Salmon into a Fishmonger's Basket; his Feet cold as Ice, his Breath hot as a Furnace, and his Hands and his Face as greasy as his Flannel Night-cap. — Oh Matrimony! — He tosses up the Clothes with a barbarous swing over his Shoulders, disorder the whole economy of my Bed, leaves me half naked, and my whole Night's Comfort is the tuneable Serenade of that wakeful Nightingale, his Nose. — O the Pleasure of counting the melancholy Clock by a snoring Husband!

Bianca Visconti, or The Heart Overtasked

Nathaniel Parker Willis

18–20
Dramatic

Fourteenth-century Milan. Bianca's father, the Duke of Milan, has just decreed that she will marry Sforza, a young nobleman with whom she has always been in love. Here, she shares the happy news with her servants.

To marry Sforza!
My dream come true! my long, long cherished dream!
The star come out of heaven that I had worshipped!
The paradise I built with soaring fancy
And filled with rapture like a honey-bee
Dropped from the clouds at last! Am I awake? —
Am I awake, dear Giulio? [. . .]
Thank God, they speak to me! It is no dream!
It was this hand my father took to tell me —
It was with these lips that I tried to speak —
It was this heart that beat its giddy prison
As if exulting joy new-sprung within it
Would out and fill the world!
Wed him tomorrow!
So suddenly a wife! [. . .] Oh, I'll tell him —
When I dare speak, I'll tell him — how I've loved him!
And day and night dreamed of him, and through all
The changing wars treasured the solemn troth
Broke by my father! If he listens kindly,

I'll tell him how I fed my eyes upon him
In Venice at his triumph — [. . .]
I was a child then — but I felt my heart
Grow, in one hour, to woman!

Bianca Visconti, or The Heart Overtasked

Nathaniel Parker Willis

18–20
Dramatic

Following her wedding to Sforza, Bianca discovers that her childish dreams of a life together won't be enough to hold the interest of a man intent on glory. Here, she vows to win his love in earnest, even if it means the death of her heart's desire.

He does not love me!
I never dreamed of this! To be his bride
Was all the heaven I looked for! Not to love me
When I have been ten years affianced to him! —
When I have lived for him — shut up my heart,
With every pulse and hope, for his use only —
Worshipped — oh, God! idolatrously loved him!
[. . .]
Why has he sought to marry me? Why still
Renew the broken pledge my father made him?
Why, for ten years, with war and policy,
Strive for my poor alliance?
[. . .]   He must love me,
Or I shall break my heart! I never had
One other hope in life! I never linked
One thought, but to this chain! I have no blood —
No breath — no being — separate from Sforza!
Nothing has any other name! The sun
Shined like his smile — the lightning was his glory —

The night his sleep, and the hushed moon watched o'er him; —
Stars writ his name — his breath hung on the flowers —
Music had no voice but to say I love him,
And life no future, but his love for me!

By Faith Alone

Marjorie Benton Cooke

40+
Comic

It's the early 1900s, and Mrs. Frederick Belmont-Towers has found a marvelous new key to enlightenment.

Is that you, Helen? Come in. You must excuse me for seeing you up here, but this is my day for treatment and I don't get up till afternoon. Oh, didn't you know? I'm taking a course with Omarkanandi, this famous Hindu priest. You haven't heard of him? Oh, my dear, he is too wonderful. You know what an invalid I've been for years? I've had no sympathy in my suffering — [. . .] but Omarkanandi says my condition has been simply pitiful! He's so sympathetic, Helen. He wears a long red robe, and a turban and the queerest rings, and his eyes are the most soulful things. Well, it's hard to tell you just what he does. He sits beside me, and holds my hands and looks into my eyes and talks to me, in his soft Oriental voice. He says he is the medium of infinite strength and power, and that he transmits it to me. Well, he thinks in time that I can draw on this power myself, without him. He says that I'm so highly strung that the winds of evil play on me. He says my chronic indigestion is simply a wind of evil, and that I must harden myself against it. I told him I didn't care so much about the indigestion itself, but it was ruining my complexion. He said when I got myself into harmony with the Infinite my skin would be like a rose leaf — so you can see for yourself the thing is worthwhile.

Cambyses, King of Persia

Thomas Preston

20–30

Dramatic

When the king's counsel, Praxaspes, criticizes the king's drinking, the enraged ruler demands that Praxaspes' young son stand at a distance so that he may shoot at him with a bow and arrow. He strikes the boy in the heart claiming that such a feat could not have been accomplished by a drunken man. Here, the boy's mother discovers his body.

O blissful babe! O joy of womb! Heart's comfort and delight!
For counsel given unto the king is this thy just requite?
O heavy day and doleful time, these mourning tunes to make!
With blubb'red eyes into mine arms from earth I will thee take
And wrap thee in mine apron white. But, O my heavy heart!
The spiteful pangs that it sustains would make it in two to part,
The death of this my son to see. Oh heavy mother now,
That from thy sweet and sug'rèd joy to sorrow so shouldst bow!
What grief in womb did I retain before I did thee see!
Yet at last, when smart was gone, what joy wert thou to me!
How tender was I of thy food, for to preserve thy state!
How stillèd I thy tender heart at times early and late!
With velvet paps I gave thee suck with issue from my breast,
And dancèd thee upon my knee to bring thee unto rest. [. . .]
Nature enforceth me, alas, in this wise to deplore,
To wring my hands. Oh wellaway, that I should see this hour!
Thy mother yet will kiss thy lips, silk-soft and pleasant white,
With wringing hands lamenting for to see thee in this plight.
My lording dear, let us go home our mourning to augment.

The Casket Comedy

Titus Maccius Plautus

Translated by Paul Nixon

35+

Comic

Halisca searches for a lost box, trusted to her by her mistress, Casina.

If heaven doesn't rescue me, I'm dead and done for, with not a soul to look to for aid! Oh, how miserable my own heedlessness makes me! Oh! how I dread what will happen to my back, if my mistress finds out I've been so negligent! Surely I had that little casket in my hands and received it from her here in front of the house — and where it is now I don't know, unless I dropped it somewhere about here, as I suspect. [. . .] Now I'll examine the footprints here, in case I can find any. For if no one passed by after I went inside, the casket would be lying here. [. . .] Track it — sharp now — like an augur! (*Looks for footprints, her nose close to the ground.*) He went this way . . . here's the mark of a shoe in the dust . . . I'll follow it up this way! Now here's where he stopped with someone else . . . [. . .] A consultation was held here . . . There are two people concerned, that's clear as day . . . Aha! Just one person's tracks! . . . He went this way . . . I'll investigate . . . From here he went over here . . . from here he went — nowhere! It's no use. What's lost is lost — the casket and my cuticle together. I'm going back inside.

The Changes of the Heart (The Double Inconstancy)

Pierre de Marivaux

Translated by Stephen Wadsworth

20s

Dramatic

Silvia is upset because she has been separated from Harlequin, whom she loves, and abducted by the prince, whom she doesn't. She takes her anger out on her servant.

Very well, my servant, you think so highly of the honor shown me here — what do I need idle ladies-in-waiting spying on me for? They take away my lover and replace him with women? Hardly adequate compensation! And what do I care about all the singing and dancing they force me to sit through? A village girl happy in a little town is worth more than a princess weeping in a gorgeous suite of rooms. If the prince is so young and beautiful and full of desire, it's not my fault. He should keep all that for his equals and leave me to my poor Harlequin, who is no more a man of means than I am a woman of leisure, who is not richer than I am or fancier than I am, and who doesn't live in a bigger house than I do, but who loves me, without guile or pretense, and whom I love in return in the same way, and for whom I will die of a broken heart if I don't see him again soon. And what have they done to him? Perhaps they are mistreating him . . . (*Silvia's rage peaks.*) I am so angry! This is so unfair! You are my servant? Get out of my sight, I cannot abide you!

The Changes of the Heart (The Double Inconstancy)

Pierre de Marivaux

Translated by Stephen Wadsworth

20s

Seriocomic

Flaminia, daughter of a palace servant, schools her coquettish sister, Lisette, on a proper winning manner.

[Y]ou must realize that anyone can see that you are bent on being [pleasing], and that just won't do. One sees it in your exquisite little hands as they wander suggestively about . . . and in those great big adorable eyes, which are so shy one moment, so rapacious the next, full of promises . . . full of ideas. And in the way you move, with a certain nonchalance, an elusive something that suggests both indifference and tenderness — your head insouciantly atilt, your chin floating lightly, your shoulders inviting the touch of a passing finger. And in the way you speak, plucking from the vine the words most apt, pausing ambiguously, and delicately building toward an extravagant flash of wit or a calculatedly rash outburst of passion. In short, you have mastered the ever so slightly dissipated elegance so de rigueur at court, which is fine here, where it is considered just the thing, and essential to the conquest of a man. But for the sake of our green country boy you'll have to do without these finer points, he simply isn't up to them. He's rather like a man who's never drunk anything but pure, clear water; absinth is hardly going to agree with him.

The Changes of Heart (The Double Inconstancy)

Pierre de Marivaux

Translated by Stephen Wadsworth

20s

Seriocomic

Silvia simply cannot understand why everyone is encouraging her to marry the prince over Harlequin, to whom she has sworn her love.

You know, this place is really dreadful. I've never seen people so . . . polite. There are so many curtseys, so many pretty speeches — you'd think they were the best people in the world, that they're full of integrity and good intentions. But no, not at all. There's not one of them who hasn't come to me and said oh-so-discreetly, "Mademoiselle, believe me, you're better off forgetting Harlequin and marrying the Prince." And they say this to me absolutely without a qualm, as if they were encouraging me to do the right thing! "But," I say to them, "I gave my promise to Harlequin. What about fidelity, honor, good faith?" They don't even know what I'm talking about. They laugh in my face and tell me I'm being childish, that a proper young lady ought to be reasonable, isn't that nice! To hold nothing sacred, to cheat one's fellow man, to go back on one's word, to be two-faced and to lie — that's how to be a proper young lady? Who are these people? Where do they come from? What dough did they make them out of?

The Cherry Orchard

Anton Chekhov

Translated by Carol Rocamora

45–55

Dramatic

Lyubov Andreevna Ranevskaya, an aristocratic landowner, speaks to her brother. Both are incapable of responding to the changing conditions around them. Lyubov instead wallows in inaction and laments the past.

I keep waiting for something to happen, as if the house were going to tumble down on top of us. [. . .]

O my sins, my sins . . . I've always thrown money around, uncontrollably, like a madwoman, and I married a man, who did nothing but keep us in debt. My husband died from too much champagne — he drank himself to death, — then, for my next misfortune, I fell in love with another man, I began living with him . . . and just at that time, there came my first great punishment, and what a blow it dealt me — right here in this river . . . my little boy drowned, and so I fled, abroad, I simply fled, never to return, never to see this river again . . . I closed my eyes and I ran, not knowing where I was going, what I was doing, and he following after . . . ruthlessly, relentlessly. I bought a dacha near Menton, he had fallen ill there, and for three years I knew no rest, neither day nor night; his illness exhausted me, wasted me, my soul withered away. And then last year, when the dacha was sold to pay off the debts, I fled again, to Paris, and there he robbed me, he left me for another woman, I tried to poison myself . . . How stupid, how shameful . . . And suddenly I felt drawn again to Russia, to my homeland, to my daughter . . . (*Wipes away her tears.*) Dear God, dear God, be merciful, forgive me my sins! Don't punish me any longer!

Children of Herakles

Euripides

Translated by Carl R. Mueller

Teens–20s

Dramatic

Exiled and sentenced to death, the young sons of Herakles flee the city of Argos with Iolaos, a kindly old man. They are taken in by the King of Athens, which brings war between the two cities. The children will be spared only if a virgin girl of noble birth is sacrificed to the gods. A Maiden steps forward, sister of the boys, and volunteers to die for her brothers.

Your fear of Argive danger is past, old man. I bring you my life. I deliver it to you of my own free will and unasked. I'm ready. Ready for sacrifice and death. The people of Athens have risked everything for us, their city, their lives, and should we, then, we who have burdened them with our miseries, shrink from death when we have the power to save them? No, it can't be, it mustn't, it would be a mockery if we who boast ourselves the children of Herakles, sat here wailing to the god for asylum, only to prove ourselves cowards, contemptible, the lowest of life, by cringing from death. What man of honor could defend such an outrage? Would it be better if this city fell, gods forbid! and I — I the daughter of a noble father — fell into the hands of the enemy, and were ravished, and died all the same, as I surely would? Or is it better I go into exile and wander away the rest of my life? [. . .] How much better it is to die than to live a fate I don't deserve, empty, meaningless. Someone else, perhaps. Not me. Not the daughter of Herakles.

Lead me now. I'm ready. [. . .] My life is yours.

Children of Herakles

Euripides
Translated by Carl R. Mueller

50s+
Dramatic

Alkmene, old mother of Herakles, is filled with hate for Eurystheus, defeated King of Argos, for trying to kill her grandchildren.

You unmerciful beast! Is this really you? Has Justice caught you at last in her net? Your head! Turn your head to face me! Have the courage at least to look your enemy in the eyes! I'm the master now, you're the slave!

Tell me — I want to know — is this the vile Eurystheus, the same Eurystheus who persecuted my son? Outrage after outrage you committed against him — wherever he is now — order after order to go out killing hydras and lions! I won't speak of the other monstrosities you devised to torment him, my tale would be too long. Was there ever once an atrocity too much for you? You even sent him down to Hades. *Live!* But not even that was enough for you. You — you pursued me and these children, hounded us throughout all of Greece, driving us from altars where we sat as suppliants, as cruelly uncaring for the old as well as the young, some of us only babies! But your misfortune was to find a city that was free, that takes pride in its freedom, and men who defend freedom at any cost. And now you'll die the death you deserve, the death of a slave. And even in that you'll be the winner, for you should die many deaths, one for every outrage you committed! (*Reaching for a weapon to strike Eurystheus.*)

The Country Wife

William Wycherly

20s

Comic

Mrs. Pinchwife struggles for a clever way to send to her would-be lover both the letter her husband would have her write, and the letter she wants to write.

For Mr. Horner — So, I am glad he has told me his name; Dear Mr. Horner, but why should I send thee such a letter, that will vex thee, and make thee angry with me? — well, I will not send it — Ay, but then my husband will kill me — for I see plainly, he won't let me love Mr. Horner — but what care I for my husband — I won't, so I won't send poor Mr. Horner such a letter — but then my husband — But oh — what if I writ at bottom, my husband made me write it — Ay, but then my husband would see't; [. . .] stay — what if I should write a letter, and wrap it up like this, and write upon't too. Ay, but then my husband would see't. I don't know what to do — But yet ye gads, I'll try, so I will — for I will not send this letter to poor Mr. Horner, come what will on't.

A Doll House

Henrik Ibsen

Translated by Rick Davis and Brian Johnston

25–30

Dramatic

Nora rejects her husband's claim that he loves her.

You've never understood me. A great wrong has been done me, Torvald. First by Papa, then by you. [. . .] You've never loved me. You just thought it was a lot of fun to be in love with me. [. . .] It's a fact, Torvald. When I was at home with Papa, he told me all his opinions; so of course I had the same opinions. And if I had any others, I kept them hidden, because he wouldn't have liked that. He called me his doll-child, and he played with me like I played with my dolls. Then I came to your house — [. . .] I mean, I went from Papa's hands into yours. You set up everything according to your taste; so of course I had the same taste, or I pretended to, I'm not really sure. I think it was half-and-half, one as much as the other. Now that I look back on it, I can see that I've lived like a beggar in this house, from hand to mouth; I've lived by doing tricks for you, Torvald. But that's how you wanted it. You and Papa have committed a great sin against me. It's your fault that I've become what I am. [. . .] You've always been very nice to me. But our home has never been anything but a playpen. I've been your doll-wife here, just like I was Papa's doll-child at home. And my children, in turn, have been my dolls. It was fun when you came and played with me, just like they had fun when I played with them. That's what our marriage has been, Torvald.

The Double Dealer

William Congreve

20s

Comic

Lady Plyant vacillates between being outraged and flattered upon learning Mellefont wants to marry her stepdaughter in order to procure her, the stepmother.

— but then, to marry my [husband's] daughter, for the conveniency of frequent opportunities [to procure me, her stepmother] — I'll never consent to that, as sure as can be, I'll break the match. Nay, nay, rise up, come, you shall see my good nature. I know love is powerful, and nobody can help his passion: I know 'tis not your fault nor I swear it is not mine. How can I help it if I have charms? And how can you help it, if you made a captive? I swear it's a pity it should be a fault — but my honor — well, but your honor, too — but the sin! — Well, but the necessity — oh, Lord, here's somebody coming, I dare not stay. Well, you must consider of your crime, and strive as much as can be against it — strive be sure — but don't be melancholy, don't despair — but never think that I'll grant you anything; oh, Lord, no; — but be sure you lay aside all thoughts of marriage, for though I know you don't love Cynthia, only as a blind for your passion to me: yet it will make me jealous — oh, Lord, what did I say? Jealous? No, no, I can't be jealous, for I must not love you — therefore, don't hope — but don't despair neither, — oh, they're coming, I must fly!

The Dutch Courtesan

John Marston

20s

Comic

Crispinella finds the act of kissing loathsome.

Pish, sister Beatrice! prithee read no more; my stomach o' late stands against kissing extremely. [. . .] By the faith and trust I bear to my face, 'tis grown one of the most unsavory ceremonies. Body o' beauty, 'tis one of the most unpleasing, injurious customs to ladies. Any fellow that has but one nose on his face, and standing collar and skirts also lined with taffety silk, must salute us on the lips as familiarly — Soft skins save us! There was a stub-bearded John-a Stile with Ployden's face saluted me last day and stuck his bristle through my lips; I ha' spent ten shilling in pomatum since to skin them again. Marry, if a nobleman or a knight with one lock visit us, though his unclean goose-turd-green teeth ha' the palsy, his nostrils smell worse than a putrefied maribone, and his loose beard drops into our bosom, yet must kiss him with a curtsy. A curse! for my part, I had as lief they would break wind in my lips.

The Dutch Courtesan

John Marston

20s

Comic

Crispinella allows her friend's husband as an exception to the otherwise tainted pool of married men.

Marry? No, faith; husbands are like lots in the lottery: you may draw forty blanks before you find one that any prize in him. A husband generally is a careless, domineering thing that grows like coral, which as long as it is under water is soft and tender, but as soon as it has got his branch above the waves is presently hard, stiff, not to be bowed but burst; so when your husband is a suitor and under your choice, Lord, how supple his is, how obsequious, how at your service, sweet lady! Once married, got up his head above, a stiff, crooked, knobby, inflexible, tyrannous creature he grows; then they turn like water: more you would embrace, the less you hold. I'll live my own woman, and if the worst come to the worst, I had rather price a wag than a fool. [. . .]

But thy match, sister, by my troth, I think 'twill do well. He's a well-shaped, clean-lipped gentleman, of a handsome but not affected fineness, a good faithful eye, and a well-humored cheek. Would he did not stoop in the shoulders, for thy sake.

The Ecclesiazusae

Aristophanes

Translator unknown

20s–30s

Comic

Praxagora, disguised as a man, makes a case for women.

[H]earken to me, you will be saved. I assert that the direction of affairs must be handed over to the women, for 'tis they who have charge and look after our households. They are worth more than you are, as I shall prove. First of all they wash all their wool in warm water, according to the ancient practice; you will never see them changing their method. Ah! if Athens only acted thus, if it did not take delight in ceaseless innovations, would not its happiness be assured? Then the women sit down to cook, as they always did; they carry things on their head as was their wont; they keep the Thesmophoria as they have ever done; they knead their cakes just as they used to; they make their husbands angry as they have always done; they receive their lovers in their houses as was their constant custom; they buy dainties as they always did; they love unmixed wine as well as ever; they delight in being loved just as much as they always have. Let us therefore hand Athens over to them without endless discussions, without bothering ourselves about what they will do; let us simply hand them over the power, remembering that they are mothers and will therefore spare the blood of our soldiers; besides, who will know better than a mother how to forward provisions to the front? Woman is adept at getting money for herself and will not easily let herself be deceived; she understands deceit too well herself. I omit a thousand other advantages. Take my advice and you will live in perfect happiness.

Elektra

Sophokles

Translated by Carl R. Mueller and Anna Krajewska-Wieczorek

30s

Dramatic

Elektra, daughter of Agamemnon and Klytaimnestra, hates her mother for murdering her father. Here, Klytaimnestra, now married to Aigisthos, argues she had good reason to do what she did.

Insolent you call me?
No. I merely return in kind
The evil taunts you always level against me.
Your father — this is your pretext, never off it! —
Was killed by me. Oh, and how right you are.
I glory in it. Justice at my side.
Justice's hand and mine brought down the ax.

And you, if you knew where your duty lay, would have helped.
This "father" you're always moaning and groaning over,
Alone among the Greeks, was brute enough
To sacrifice your sister to the gods;
That "father" who knew nothing of the pangs
I suffered in giving her birth.

Tell me this: Why did he sacrifice her?
Who was he trying to please?
The Greeks, you'll say.
But what right had they to slay my child? [. . .]

Callous, perverse excuse for a father!
Or so I see it. Whatever you may think!
And so would my dead child if she could speak.
What I have done was done without regret.
But if you call me evil, first make certain
Your own judgment is sound before you condemn.

Elektra

Sophokles

Translated by Carl R. Mueller and Anna Krajewska-Wieczorek

30s

Dramatic

Elektra, daughter of Klytaimnestra and Agamemnon, hates her mother for killing her father. But Klytaimnestra claims the murder was just, as Agamemnon slaughtered another daughter in sacrifice to the gods. Still, Elektra doesn't let her mother off the hook.

You killed my father, you say.
What word could bring you greater shame than that,
Whether you did it justly or unjustly?
I maintain that your deed was not just;
That you were seduced to it by the wooing
Of the evil man whose bed you now share. [. . .]

Tell me you are not committing the most shameful of acts:
Cohabiting with him whose hands are blood-stained
With my father's murder,
With whom you first laid plans to kill my father,
And breed with him children you cherish more
Than the lawful children you bore in lawful marriage,
Whom now you cast off from your love. [. . .]

But I haven't even the right to rebuke you.
You'd shriek I'm reviling my mother.
Mother! You're no mother!
You're a jailer who makes my life wretched
With all the miseries you cast at me,
You and your bedmate in crime!

Enemies

Maxim Gorky

35+

Dramatic

Tatiana, an actress, is in a creative slump.

I did once think that on the stage my feet were planted in solid ground . . . That I might grow tall . . . (*Emphatically, with distress.*) But now it's all so painful — I feel uncomfortable up there in front of those people, with their cold eyes saying, "Oh, we know all that, it's old, it's boring!" I feel weak and defenseless in front of them, I can't capture them, I can't excite them . . . I long to tremble in front of them with fear, with joy, to speak words full of fire and passion and anger, words that cut like knives, that burn like torches . . . I want to throw armfuls of words, throw them bounteously, abundantly, terrifyingly . . . So that people are set alight by them and shout aloud, and turn to flee from them . . . And then I'll stop them. Toss them different words. Words beautiful as flowers. Words full of hope and joy, and love. And they'll all be weeping, and I'll weep too . . . wonderful tears. They applaud. Smother me with flowers. Bear me up on their shoulders. For a moment — I hold sway over them all . . . Life is there, in that one moment, all of life, in a single moment. Everything that's best is always in a single moment.

Eumenides

Aeschylus

Translated by Carl R. Mueller

20s–30s

Dramatic

The goddess Athena absolves Orestes for the murder of his mother and incurs the wrath of the Furies. She persuades the Furies to accept the verdict, then urges them to sing for peace and the future of Athens.

Sing of victory —
a song of victory with honor.
Sing of the earth and the sea and the
blessings they give; of the sky and gentle
rain, and of soft winds blowing the
land on sun-drenched days,
sing of these blessings.
Sing of the beasts of the fields, of endless
herds and of grain-rich harvests,
abundance of earth's fruits,
blessings unending,
sing of them,
of their blessings,
for our city's people,
blessings that will know no end.
And sing of the preservation of human seed,
the sowing of new life, and piety
cultivated to make the good man thrive.
For like a loving gardener, I tend the good and
pluck out the bad, and save the honest man
from sorrow.

All these are yours,
            these gifts of peace. My task is to
            tend the arts of war, to see that this
city is forever honored
by bringing her glorious victory in battle. [. . .]

Our rivalry now will be for good,
and Athens will be
blest in our contest.

The Faithful Shepherd

Giambattista Guarini
Translator unknown

16–20
Dramatic

After she has sent her lover Mirtillo away, Amarillis laments their impossible love for one another.

Mirtillo, O Mirtillo, couldst thou see
That heart which thou condemn'st of cruelty
— Soul of my soul! — thou unto it wouldst show
That pity which thou begst from it, I know.
Oh ill-starred lovers! what avails it me
To have thy love! T'have mine, what boots it thee?
Whom love hath joined why dost thou separate,
Malicious fate? And two divorced by fate
Why joinst thou, perverse love? How blest are you
Wild beasts that are in loving tied unto
No laws but those of love! whilst human laws
Inhumanly condemn us for that cause.
Oh why, if this be such a natural
And powerful passion, was it capital? [. . .]
Ah, my Mirtillo, would to heaven that were
The only penalty!

Fatal Curiosity

George Lillo

30s

Seriocomic

Agnes, a poor woman, steals jewels from the casket of a dead man.

Why should my curiosity excite me
To search and pry into th'affairs of others,
Who have t'employ my thoughts so many cares
And sorrows of my own? With how much ease
The spring gives way! Surprising! Most prodigious!
My eyes are dazzled and my ravished heart
Leaps at the glorious sight. How bright's the lustre,
How immense the worth of these fair jewels!
Aye, such a treasure would expel forever
Base poverty and all its abject train:
The mean devices we're reduced to use
To keep famine and preserve our lives
From day to day, the cold neglect of friends,
The galling scorn or more provoking pity
Of an insulting world. Possessed of these,
Plenty, content, and power might take their turn,
And lofty pride bare its aspiring head
At our approach and once more bend before us.
A pleasing dream! — 'Tis past, and now I wake
More wretched by the happiness I've lost.
For sure it was a happiness to think
Though but a moment, such a treasure mine.
Nay it was more than thought. I saw and touched
The bright temptation, and I see it yet.
'Tis here — 'tis mine — I have it in possession!

Gallathea

John Lyly

20s

Dramatic

When Diana, goddess of the hunt, discovers that her virgin nymphs have all fallen in love, she lectures them on the importance of remaining chaste.

Your chaste hearts, my nymphs, should resemble the onyx, which is hottest when it is whitest, and your thoughts, the more they are assaulted with desires, the less they should be affected. [. . .] Of all trees the cedar is greatest and hath the smallest seeds; of all affections love hath the greatest name and the least virtue. Shall it be said, and shall Venus say it, nay, shall it be seen, and shall wantons see it, that Diana, the goddess of chastity, whose thoughts are always answerable to her vows, whose eyes never glanced on desire, and whose heart abateth the point of Cupid's arrows, shall have her virgins to become unchaste in desires, immoderate in affection, untemperate in love, in foolish love, in base love? [. . .] O my dear nymphs, if you knew how loving thoughts stain lovely faces, you would be as careful to have the one as unspotted as the other beautiful. [. . .] I blush, ladies, that you, having been heretofore patient of labors, should now become prentices to idleness, and use the pen for sonnets, not the needle for samplers. And how is your love placed? Upon pelting boys, perhaps base of birth, without doubt weak of discretion. Ay, but they are fair. O ladies, do your eyes begin to love colors, whose hearts was wont to loath them? Is Diana's chase become Venus' court, and are your holy vows turned to hollow thoughts?

A Glass of Water

Eugene Scribe

Translated by Robert Cornthwaite

30s–40s

Dramatic

Upon being pressured by a journalist into hiring a shop girl to assist the queen, the Duchess parries, proving herself a formidable force.

(*Proudly.*) Whether or not she's my relative will not affect my decision. As for you, my lord, a journalist — and especially an opposition journalist — before he meddles in State affairs, should put his own affairs in order. You have enormous debts, which your creditors have sold me at fifteen percent on the pound. I've bought them all. (*Smiling.*) These debts of yours could lead to your imprisonment, something I have never done to a member of the House of Commons — at least not yet. Now, if the piquant story you mention should appear in your paper tomorrow morning, the evening journal will announce that its brilliant author is at that moment in Newgate prison. But I am sure you will see the wisdom of keeping quiet. (*She makes a reverence and leaves.*)

Hey for Honesty

Thomas Randolph

40–50

Seriocomic

The aging and disgruntled Anus bemoans the fact that men seem to prefer younger women.

Heigho! methinks I am sick with lying alone last night. Well, I will scratch out the eyes of this same rascally Plutus, god of wealth, that has undone me. Alas! poor woman, since the shop of Plutus his eyes has been open, what abundance of misery has befallen thee! Now the young gallant will no longer kiss thee nor embrace thee; but thou, poor widow, must lie comfortless in a solitary pair of sheets, having nothing to cover thee but the lecherous rug and the bawdy blankets. O, that I were young again! how it comforts me to remember the death of my maidenhead! Alas! poor woman, they contemn old age, as if our lechery was out of date. They say we are cold: methinks that thought should make 'um take compassion of us, and lie with us — if not for love, for charity. They say we are dry: so much the more capable of Cupid's fire; while young wenches, like green wood, smoke before they flame. They say we are old: why, then, experience makes us more expert. They tell us our lips are wrinkled: why that in kissing makes the sweeter titillation. They swear we have no teeth: why, then, they need not fear biting. Well, if our lease of lechery be out, yet methinks we might purchase a night-labourer for his day's wages. I will be revenged of this same Plutus, that wrongs the orphans, and is so uncharitable to the widows.

Hippolytus

Euripides

Translated by Carl R. Mueller

30s+

Dramatic

Phaidra, a married woman with children, is under Aphrodite's spell; she is hopelessly in love with Hippolytus and so ashamed of herself she wants to die. Here, her nurse tries to reason with her.

All right now, my dear! Let's just put it aside, this, this wrong-headedness of yours, this talk of suicide. For that's what it is. Conceit. It's conceited to think that you can fight the gods on their own turf and win. Be brave. Give in to it. [. . .]

More than a few, dearie — and all of them perfectly sensible men — happily give in to this state of affairs. Avoid a scandal and who really cares. Oh, there are husbands in abundance who, catching their wives sneaking off with the latest lover, will turn a blind eye. And fathers who pimp for their rowdy sons, shoving some soft young miss into his steamy bed. It's a wise maxim that says: "Ignorance is bliss." But there's just no sense in striving for too much perfection. It's like the roof of a house. Only fools demand perfection where it won't be seen. Sex is a rough and stormy sea, how can you expect to swim to safety? No, dear. The best any of us can hope for — and it's not to be sneezed at — is to end our lives with a little more good than bad in our balance.

Hyde Park

James Shirley

30s

Comic

Mistress Carol extols the virtues of the single life.

You do intend to marry him, then?
What is in your condition makes you weary?
You are sick of plenty and command; you have
Too, too much liberty, too many servants;
Your jewels are your own, and you would see
How they will show upon your husband's wagtail.
You have a coach now, and a Christian livery
To wait on you to church, and are not catechised
When you come home; you have a waiting woman,
A monkey, squirrel, and a brace of islands,
Which may be thought superfluous in your family
When husbands come to rule. A pretty wardrobe,
A tailor of your own, a doctor, too,
[. . .] You have the benefit
Of talking loud and idle at your table,
May sing a wanton ditty, and not be chid;
Dance and go late to bed, say your own prayers,
And you will lose all this, for
"I, Cicely, take thee, John, to be my husband?"
Keep him still to be your servant;
Imitate me; a hundred suitors cannot
Be half the trouble of one husband.

An Ideal Husband

Oscar Wilde

20s

Comic

Mabel Chiltern wishes Tommy would get it right.

Well, Tommy has proposed to me again. Tommy really does nothing but propose to me. He proposed to me last night in the music-room, when I was quite unprotected, as there was an elaborate trio going on. I didn't dare to make the smallest repartee, I need hardly tell you. If I had, it would have stopped the music at once. [. . .] Then he proposed to me in broad daylight this morning, in front of that dreadful statue of Achilles. Really, the things that go on in front of that work of art are quite appalling. The police should interfere. At luncheon I saw by the glare in his eye that he was going to propose again, and I just managed to check him in time by assuring him that I was a bimetallist. Fortunately I don't know what bimetallism means. And I don't believe anybody else does either. But the observation crushed Tommy for ten minutes. [. . .] I am very fond of Tommy, but his methods of proposing are quite out of date. I wish, Gertrude, you would speak to him, and tell him that once a week is quite often enough to propose to any one, and that it should always be done in a manner that attracts some attention.

The Importance of Being Earnest

Oscar Wilde

45+

Comic

Lady Bracknell implores Algernon to dispense with petty annoyances in preparation for her upcoming party.

Well, I must say, Algernon, that I think it is high time that Mr. Bunbury made up his mind whether he was going to live or die. This shilly-shallying with the question is absurd. Nor do I in any way approve of the modern sympathy with invalids. I consider it morbid. Illness of any kind is hardly a thing to be encouraged in others. Health is the primary duty of life. I am always telling that to your poor uncle, but he never seems to take much notice . . . as far as any improvement in his ailment goes. Well, Algernon, of course if you are obliged to be beside the bedside of Mr. Bunbury, I have nothing more to say. But I would be much obliged if you would ask Mr. Bunbury, from me, to be kind enough not to have a relapse on Saturday, for I rely on you to arrange my music for me. It is my last reception, and one wants something that will encourage conversation, particularly at the end of the season when every one has practically said whatever they had to say, which, in most cases, was probably not much.

It's a Family Affair — We'll Settle It Ourselves

Alexander Ostrovsky
Translated by George Rapall Noyes

20+
Comic

The awkward Lipochka imagines the ideal dancing partner.

What a pleasant occupation these dances are! Very good indeed! What could be more delightful? You go to the assembly, or to somebody's wedding, you sit down, naturally, all beflowered like a doll or a magazine picture. Suddenly up runs a gentleman: "May I have the happiness, miss?" Well, you see, if he's a man of wit, or a military individual, you accept, drop your eyes a little, and answer: "If you please, with pleasure!" Ah! (*Warmly.*) Most fas-ci-nat-ing! Simply beyond understanding! (*Sighs.*) I dislike most of all dancing with students and government office clerks. But it's the real thing to dance with army men! Ah, charming! Ravishing! Their mustaches, and epaulets, and uniforms, and on some of them even spurs with little bits of bells. [. . .] Now, what comparison can there be between a soldier and a civilian? A soldier! Why, you can see right off his cleverness and everything. But what does a civilian amount to? Just a dummy.

Ivanov

Anton Chekhov
Translated by Carol Rocamora

30+
Dramatic

Anna Petrovna loves her husband, though he treats her poorly. Ill, she speaks about him to her doctor.

I'm beginning to think, doctor, that fate has cheated me. The majority of people, who may be no better than I, still have experienced happiness and have not had to pay for it. I have paid for it all, for all of it! . . . And how dearly! Why must I pay such a terrible price? . . . My dear friend, you are so careful with me, so gentle, you're afraid to tell the truth, but don't you think I know what my illness is? I know very well. However, it's so depressing to talk about it . . . (*In a Jewish accent.*) Hekscuse, pleez! Can you tell me a joke? [. . .]

Nikolai can. And, you know, I'm also beginning to be astonished by the unfairness of others: Why don't people respond to love with love, why do they reward truth with lies? Tell me: How much longer will my parents continue to despise me? They live roughly sixty miles from here, and day and night I feel their hatred, even in my dreams. And how am I supposed to take this depression of Nikolai's? He tells me he no longer loves me, but only in the evenings, when his anxiety oppresses him. This I understand, this I can tolerate, only imagine if he were to stop loving me entirely! Of course, this is impossible — but what if it were to happen all of a sudden? No, no, I must not even think of it. (*Sings.*)"Little finch, little finch, where have you been? . . ."(*Shudders.*) What terrible thoughts torment me! . . . You're not a family man, doctor, you wouldn't understand most of this . . .

John Gabriel Borkman

Henrik Ibsen

Translated by Rick Davis and Brian Johnston

30s

Dramatic

1896. Ella, sister of Gunhild, confronts her sister's husband over a past betrayal.

Murderer! You've committed the great, mortal sin. Do you understand what that means? The Bible speaks of a mysterious sin for which there can be no forgiveness. I've never been able to grasp what that could be. But now I see. The great, unforgivable sin is to murder someone's ability to love. That's what you've done. I never understood what happened to me until tonight. When you deserted me and turned instead to Gunhild — I thought it was just ordinary weakness on your part, and heartless scheming on hers. And I almost think I despised you a little, in spite of everything. But now I see it! You betrayed the woman you loved! Me, me, me! You were ready to trade the thing you held dearest for the sake of profit. And so you've committed a double murder! Your own soul — and mine! [. . .]

King Lear

William Shakespeare

30s

Dramatic

Goneral is tired of her aging father's behaviors. She speaks to her steward, Oswald.

By day and night he wrongs me; every hour
He flashes into one gross crime or other,
That sets us all at odds: I'll not endure it:
His knights grow riotous, and himself upbraids us
On every trifle. When he returns from hunting,
I will not speak with him; say I am sick:
If you come slack of former services,
You shall do well; the fault of it I'll answer.

[. . .]

Put on what weary negligence you please,
You and your fellows; I'll have it come to question:
If he dislike it, let him to our sister,
Whose mind and mine, I know, in that are one,
Not to be over-ruled. Idle old man,
That still would manage those authorities
That he hath given away! Now, by my life,
Old fools are babes again; and must be used
With cheques as flatteries, — when they are seen abused.
Remember what I tell you.

The Lady from the Sea

Henrik Ibsen

Translated by Rick Davis and Brian Johnston

20s–30s

Dramatic

1877. Ellida is determined to break away from her controlling husband for an ex-lover.

You can't prevent me choosing — not you nor anyone else. You can forbid me to go away with him — to follow him — if that's what I choose. You can keep me here by force, against my will. You can do that. But as to my choosing — from my inmost heart — choosing him and not you — if I should want to — that's something you can't prevent. And besides, I've nothing whatever to stand in my way. No earthly tie here at home to compel and hold me. I've no roots whatever in this house, Wangel. The children don't belong to me — not in their hearts, I mean. They've never belonged. When I go away — if I go away — either with him tonight or else out to Skjoldvik tomorrow, I won't even have a key to hand over — not an instruction to leave behind about anything at all. That's how completely rootless I've been in this house, how completely an outsider from the beginning. [. . .] Now there's no compelling reason, nothing to hold me, or help me stay — (*Clenching her hands in anxiety and distress.*) And now, tonight, in half an hour, he'll be here, the man I betrayed, the man I should have held to as faithfully as he's held to me.

The Lady of Pleasure

James Shirley

18–25

Seriocomic

Celestina, a wealthy and crafty young widow, reveals her secret for attracting men.

One thing I'll tell you more, and this I give you
Worthy of your imitation from my practice:
You see me merry, full of song and dancing,
Pleasant in language, apt to all delights
That crown a public meeting, but you cannot
Accuse me of being prodigal of my favours
To any of my guests. I do not summon
(By any wink) a gentleman to follow me
To my withdrawing chamber; I hear all
Their pleas in court; nor can they boast abroad
(And do me justice) after a salute
They have much conversation with my lip.
I hold the kissing of my hand a courtesy,
And he that loves me must, upon the strength
Of that, expect till I renew his favour.
Some ladies are so expensive in their graces
To those that honour 'em, and so prodigal,
That in a little time they have nothing but
The naked sin left to reward their servants;
Whereas a thrift in our rewards will keep
Men long in their devotion, and preserve
Our selves in stock, to encourage those that honour us. [. . .]

It takes not from the freedom of our mirth,
But seems to advance it, when we can possess
Our pleasures with security of our honour;
And that preserved, I welcome all the joys
My fancy can let in. In this I have given
The copy of my mind, nor do I blush
You understand it.

Lady Windermere's Fan

Oscar Wilde

45+

Comic

Amid a crazy quilt of gossip, the Duchess of Berwick implores her sister-in-law to get Windermere out of town, for his association with a "terrible" woman is causing a scandal.

My dear nieces — you know the Saville girls, don't you? — such nice domestic creatures — plain, dreadfully plain, — but so good — well, they're always at the window doing fancy work, and making ugly things for the poor, which I think so useful of them in these dreadful socialistic days, and this terrible woman has taken a house in Curzon Street, right opposite them — such a respectable street, too! I don't know what we're coming to! And they tell me that Windermere goes there four and five times a week — they *see* him. They can't help it — and although they never talk scandal, they — well, of course — they remark on it to every one. And the worst of it all is that I have been told that this woman has got a great deal of money out of somebody, for it seems that she came to London six months ago without anything at all to speak of, and now she has this charming house in Mayfair, drives her ponies in the park every afternoon and all — well, all — since she has known poor dear Windermere. It's quite true, my dear. The whole of London knows about it. That is why I felt it was better to come and talk to you, and advise you to take Windermere away at once to Homburg or to Aix, where he'll have something to amuse him, and where you can watch him all day long.

La Ronde

Arthur Schnitzler

Translated by Carl R. Mueller

25–30

Dramatic

Emilie's husband-to-be cannot bear to hear the truth about her past, even though he claims to love her. Emile lashes out at the unfairness of his position.

Women who can lie are so fortunate. No. You men can't bear to deal with the truth. I want to know: Why did you always beg me to tell you? Oh, I can hear you say it: "I'll forgive you everything! Everything! But a lie!" And I! Who confessed everything to you! Who crawled at your feet like a kicked animal! And cried out to you: "Anatol, I'm not worthy of you, but I love you!" I gave you none of the silly excuses others give. No. I said it straight out: "Anatol, I've lived a dissolute life, I was hot-blooded, I lusted, I sold myself, I gave myself away. I'm not worthy of your love." And do you remember? I told you this before you kissed my hand for the first time. I wanted to escape you. Because I loved you so much. And you pursued me. You begged for my love. And I didn't want you. Because I didn't want to degrade the man I loved more, and differently than — oh, God, the first man I ever loved! And you took me. And I was yours! And you lifted me up so high. And gave me back everything, piece by piece, that they had taken from me. In your passionate arms I became what I had never been. Pure. Happy. You were so noble. You forgave me. And now? And now you're turning me out again. Because I'm like all the others.

Lena

Ludovico Ariosto

Translator uknown

20–30

Seriocomic

Italy. Lena, a high-strung and selfish woman, has been having an affair with Fazio. When the lovers quarrel over money, Fazio ends the affair. Here, Lena rages against being dumped by her lover.

(*Soliloquizing.*) My God, he does want things all his own way! He thinks he can poison me with his stinking breath, ride me to exhaustion like a damned donkey, and then reward me with a "Thank you very much!" A fine young gallant he is, to make a girl want to give him something for nothing! Oh! I was a silly woman to listen to his stories and his promises in the first place. But my useless brute of a husband kept on at me about it, till I thought he'd never stop. "My dear, you'd better do what he wants. It'll make our fortune! If you know how to handle him, he'll pay all our debts." And anyone would have believed it to begin with. He promised us the earth and all that therein is, as these scholars say. Well, he laid a trap for us, and I hope to see him break his own neck in it. Since he won't keep all those promises, I'm going to behave like servants do when their wages aren't paid — they get their own back on their masters by cheating them, robbing them and murdering them. And I'm going to get paid somehow, too, and I'll do anything, whether it's right or wrong. And no one can blame me for it — neither god nor man. If Fazio had a wife, I'd put all my efforts into making him a . . . , a . . . — what he's made Pacifico. But that's impossible, because his wife's dead; so I'll make him a . . . — what I said before — through his daughter.

The Libation Bearers

Aeschylus

Translated by Carl R. Mueller

20s

Dramatic

Elektra is ecstatic that her brother, Orestes, has returned home, as the palace is stained with the blood of their sister and father.

O dearest, dearest darling of your father's
house!
How much I've hoped, how much I've
wept,
the seed to renew this house!
You'll win it back, you will,
your father's house! Your
strength will win it back!
Orestes bright light of this house,
I have four loves to give you!
The love for a father,
for that's what you are to me now;
the love I should have for my mother —
the woman I so justly hate,
despise;
the love I had for my sister, ruthlessly
slaughtered; and the love that's only your own,
the love for a brother,
mine, my own,
who loved and honored me!
O Orestes!

A Live Woman in the Mines, or Pike County Ahead!

"Old Block" Alonzo Delano

20s

Seriocomic

1857: Outside the mountains of Sacramento, miner High Betty Marlin searches for her man. She has received a letter from her love, Jess, and makes up her mind to follow him into the California wilderness. She is soon lost in the mountains.

(*Sitting down on a rock.*) O, dear, what trouble I have in hunting up a man — come two-thousand miles and havn't found him yet; ef it had been any body else but Jess, I'd seen all the men hung first, afore I'd wore out so much shoe-leather in running arter 'em! Ef it hadn't been for him, I'd have been hoein' corn and pulling flax on the plantation now, instead of climbing these hills. These pesky men do bother our heads so orfully when they do get in; thar's no getting along without one — and after all thar isn't one in a hundred that's worth the trouble they give us. Then, like a flea, thar's no sartinty of catching one — for just as yer get yer finger on him, like as any way he's hopping off after somebody else. Let me catch Jess hoppin' arter somebody else. Giminy! wouldn't I give him jessie? — wouldn't I crack him? O, Jess, Jess — you run arter somebody else! O, murder! O, ef he should? O! O! (*Weeps.*) I'm a poor, lone, lorn woman — Uncle Joe sick — lost in the mountains — and Jess, my Jess, to serve me so! My courage is gone — my boots worn out — wagon tire getting loose — my best har comb broke — all trying to find a man, and him to use me so. (*Weeps.*) It will break my heart! O! O! O! (*A gun shot is heard.*) Ha! [. . .] (*Forgets her lamentation instantly; runs to the wagon and seizes a rifle.*) Keep still, Uncle Joe — ef thar's danger, I'm ready for it.

A Looking Glass for London and England

Thomas Lodge and Robert Greene

20s

Seriocomic

Remilia, vain Princess of Assyria, encourages her ladies-in-waiting to praise her beauty.

Fair Queens, yet handmaids unto Rasni's love,
Tell me, is not my state as glorious
As Juno's pomp when, 'tired with heaven's despoil,
Clad in her vestments, spotted all with stars,
She crossed the silver path unto her Jove?
Is not Remilia far more beauteous,
Riched with the pride of nature's excellence,
Than Venus in the brightest of her shine?
My hairs, surpass they not Apollo's locks?
Are not my tresses curlèd with such art
As love delights to hide him in their fair?
Doth not mine eye shine like the morning lamp
That tells Aurora when her love will come?
Have I not stol'n the beauty of the heavens
And placed it on the feature of my face?
Can any goddess make compare with me,
Or match her with the fair Remilia? [. . .]
Shut close these curtains straight and shadow me
For fear Apollo spy me in his walks,
And scorn all eyes to see Remilia's eyes.
Nymphs, eunuchs, sing, for Mavors draweth nigh.
Hide me in closure, let him long to look,
For were a goddess fairer than am I,
I'll scale the heavens to pull her from the place.

Lysistrata

Aristophanes

Translator unknown

30s

Seriocomic

The Chorus of Women lays it on the line for the graybeards.

What matters that I was born a woman, if I can cure your misfortunes? I pay my share of tolls and taxes, by giving men to the State. But you, you miserable greybeards, you contribute nothing to the public charges; on the contrary, you have wasted the treasure of our forefathers, as it was called, the treasure amassed in the days of the Persian Wars. You pay nothing at all in return; and into the bargain you endanger our lives and liberties by your mistakes. Have you one word to say for yourselves? [. . .] Ah! don't irritate me, you there, or I'll lay my slipper across your jaws; and it's pretty heavy. By the blessed goddesses, if you anger me, I will let loose the beast of my evil passions, and a very hailstorm of blows will set you yelling for help. Come, dames, off tunics, and quick's the word; women must scent the savour of women in the throes of passion. [. . .] Now just you dare to measure strength with me, old greybeard, and I warrant you you'll never eat garlic or black beans more. No, not a word! My anger is at a boiling point, and I'll do with you what the beetle did with the eagle's eggs. I laugh at your threats, so long as I have on my side Lampita here, and the noble Theban, my dear Ismenia. [. . .] Pass decree on decree, you can do us no hurt, you wretch abhorred of all your fellows. [. . .] We shall never cease to suffer the like, till someone gives you a neat trip-up and breaks your neck for you!

Macbeth

William Shakespeare

30–45

Dramatic

Lady Macbeth steels herself for the task at hand.

The raven himself is hoarse
That croaks the fatal entrance of Duncan
Under my battlements. Come, you spirits
That tend on mortal thoughts, unsex me here,
And fill me from the crown to the toe top-full
Of direst cruelty! make thick my blood;
Stop up the access and passage to remorse,
That no compunctious visitings of nature
Shake my fell purpose, nor keep peace between
The effect and it! Come to my woman's breasts,
And take my milk for gall, you murdering ministers,
Wherever in your sightless substances
You wait on nature's mischief! Come, thick night,
And pall thee in the dunnest smoke of hell,
That my keen knife see not the wound it makes,
Nor heaven peep through the blanket of the dark,
To cry "Hold, hold!"

A Mad World, My Masters

Thomas Middleton

20–30

Seriocomic

London. Here, the brassy courtesan tells another woman how to make her husband jealous.

When husbands in their rank'st suspicions dwell,
Then 'tis our best art to dissemble well.
Put but these notes in use that I'll direct you
He'll curse himself that e'er he did suspect you.
Perhaps he will solicit you, as in trial,
To visit such and such: still give denial.
Let no persuasions sway you; they are but fetches
Set to betray you, jealousies, slights, and reaches.
Seem in his sight to endure the sight of no man;
Put by all kisses, till you kiss in common;
Neglect all entertain; if he bring in
Strangers, keep you your chamber, be not seen;
If he chance steal upon you, let him find
Some book lie open 'gainst an unchaste mind,
And coted scriptures, though for your own pleasure
You read some stirring pamphlet, and convey it
Under your skirt, the fittest place to lay it.
This is the course, my wench, to enjoy thy wishes;
Here you perform best when you most neglect;
The way to daunt is to outvie suspect.
Manage these principles but with art and life,
Welcome all nations, thou'rt an honest wife.

Madame Fickle

Thomas Durfey

20s

Comic

Madame Fickle employs her wiles.

Ha, ha, ha, ha —
That heaven should give man so proud a heart,
And yet so little knowledge — silly creature,
That talks, and laughs, and kisses oft that hand
That steals away its reason as if nature
Had played the traitor and seduced the sex,
Without the aid of destiny, or women.
Ah, with what pleasant ease
The bird may be ensnared — Set but a wanton look,
You catch whole coveys; nay there is magic
Pertaining to our sex, that draws 'em in,
Though in the long vacation — and by heaven,
I am resolved to work my sly deceits
Till my revenge is perfect — thus far I've done well,
And I'll persevere in the mystery,
Wheedle 'em to the snare with cunning plots;
Then bring it off with quick designing wit,
And quirks of dubious meaning. Turn and wind
Like fox, in a storm, to prey on all,
And yet be thought a saint — thus queen I'll sit,
And hell shall laugh to see a woman's wit.

The Maid's Tragedy

Beaumont and Fletcher

20s

Dramatic

The King of Rhodes has forced young Amnitor to renounce his beloved Aspatia to marry Evadne, the king's secret mistress. On their wedding night, Evadne confesses her affair with the king to Amnitor and begs his forgiveness.

My lord,
Give me your griefs: You are an innocent,
A soul as white as heaven; let not my sins
Perish your noble youth. I do not fall here
To shadow, by dissembling with my tears,
(As, all say, women can), or to make less,
What my hot will hath done, which Heaven and you
Know to be tougher than the hand of time
Can cut from man's remembrance. No, I do not:
I do appear the same, the same Evadne,
Drest in the shames I lived in: the same monster!
But these are names of honour, to what I am:
I do present myself the foulest creature,
Most poisonous, dangerous, and despised of men,
Lerna e'er bred, or Nilus! I am hell,
Till you, my dear lord, shoot your light into me,
The beams of your forgiveness. I am soulsick,
And wither with the fear of one condemn'd,
Till I have got your pardon.

Medeia

Euripides

Translated by Carl R. Mueller

30s

Dramatic

Rather than subject her children to a life of exile, or allow them to be raised by another woman, Medeia decides to kill them. But when the time comes, she vacillates.

Without you, my dears, my life will be one of grief, gray and tedious with pain and misery. Your kind, warm eyes will never see me again, for you will pass into another place where I am forbidden to follow. Ah, why are you looking at me like that? Oh my dears, why smile this last smile?

AIIIIIII! What can I do? My heart melts when I see their bright faces! I can't! I can't! [. . .] Farewell, plans!

I'll take them, my boys, take them from the land! Out of Korinth! Why should I give pain to them to pain their father and double my own pain with greater grief! I won't do it, I won't! Farewell, my plans! No, but what — what am I saying? What's come over me? What is it? Am I to let my enemies go unpunished and make myself a laughing-stock for their mockery? How can I allow my heart such shameful weakness?

Children! Into the house now! My hand will never hesitate. Ah! Ah, no! I can't! Can't do it! Can't! You mustn't! mustn't! mustn't do these things! Let them go, spare them, they will live with you in Athens, make you happy. No, no, I can never, never by all the Furies in Hades, leave my children to my enemies to humiliate! Never. There's only one answer. They die.

Medeia

Euripides

Translated by Carl R. Mueller

30s

Dramatic

Medeia, wife of Jason, must bear the humiliation of watching her husband take another wife. Fearing Medeia may take revenge, King Kreon has given her one day before she is exiled. Medeia plots to make the most of her time.

I have so many ways of making their deaths, I don't know which to choose.

Shall I set fire to the bridal chamber, or, creeping to their bed, knife them in the gut? But it's not so simple. If they catch me trying to enter the palace and plotting its destruction, they will kill me, and then my enemies will laugh. No. The direct way is best. Poison. And it is the best of my skills. So be it. But then what? When they are dead? What city will take me in? [. . .] None. I'll wait. Just a while. And if some bastion of safety should appear, I will carry out the murders with silent cunning. But if Fate forces my hand into the open, then, steeling my heart to the utmost, I will take the sword, although it mean my death, and kill them. [. . .]

Come, Medeia! Time to breed plans. Use all your skills. Set your mind to the task. Now comes the test of your courage. Look how you are abused. By what right does Jason and his Sisyphean mob mock you, a king's daughter, whose grandsire was the Sun? No need to think now. Act. For what are we but women; incapable of noble action; skilled architects of every evil?

A Midsummer Night's Dream

William Shakespeare

30+
Comic

Titania wakes and, under Oberon's spell, falls hopelessly in love with Bottom, upon whom Puck has fixed a donkey's head.

Out of this wood do not desire to go:
Thou shalt remain here, whether thou wilt or no.
I am a spirit of no common rate;
The summer still doth tend upon my state;
And I do love thee: therefore go with me.
I'll give thee fairies to attend on thee;
And they shall fetch thee jewels from the deep,
And sing, while thou on pressed flowers dost sleep:
Peaseblossom! Cobweb! Moth! and Mustardseed!
Be kind and courteous to this gentleman;
Feed him with apricocks and dewberries,
With purple grapes, green figs, and mulberries;
And pluck the wings from painted butterflies
To fan the moonbeams from his sleeping eyes.
Nod to him, elves, and do him courtesies.

The Misanthrope

Molière

Translated by Henri van Laun

20s

Comic

Célimène extols the nonvirtues of a boorish guest.

Poor silly woman, and the dreariest company! When she comes to visit me, I suffer from martyrdom; one has to rack one's brain perpetually to find out what to say to her; and the impossibility of her expressing her thoughts allows the conversation to drop every minute. In vain you try to overcome her stupid silence by the assistance of the most commonplace topics; even the fine weather, the rain, the heat and the cold are subjects, which, with her, are soon exhausted. Yet for all that, her calls, unbearable enough, are prolonged to an insufferable length; and you may consult the clock, or yawn twenty times, but she stirs no more than a log of wood.

Mrs. Warren's Profession

George Bernard Shaw

40s

Dramatic

1893, England. Mrs. Warren, a hardworking madam, has supported her daughter, Vivie, by managing prostitutes. When Vivie discovers the truth about her mother's profession, she is sympathetic. Here, Mrs. Warren makes no apologies for her chosen career.

Well, of course, dearie, it's only good manners to be ashamed of it: its expected from a woman. Women have to pretend to feel a great deal that they don't feel. Liz used to be angry with me for plumping out the truth about it. She used to say that when every woman could learn enough from what was going on in the world before her eyes, there was no need to talk about it to her. But then Liz was such a perfect lady! She had the true instinct of it; while I was always a bit of a vulgarian. I used to be so pleased when you sent me your photos to see that you were growing up like Liz: you've just her ladylike, determined way. But I can't stand saying one thing when everyone knows I mean another. What's the use in such hypocrisy? If people arrange the world that way for women, there's no good pretending it's arranged the other way. No: I never was a bit ashamed really. I consider I had a right to be proud of how we managed everything so respectably, and never had a word against us, and how the girls were so well taken care of. Some of them did very well: one of them married an ambassador. But of course now I daren't talk about such things: whatever would they think of us! (*She yawns.*) Oh dear! I do believe I'm getting sleepy after all. (*She stretches herself lazily, thoroughly relieved by her explosion, and placidly ready for her night's rest.*)

Mrs. Warren's Profession

George Bernard Shaw

40s

Dramatic

1893, England. When Vivie discovers that her mother is still a working madam, she angrily announces her intention to sever all ties with her. Here, Mrs. Warren does her best to point out to idealistic Vivie that life is hard, and to survive, you need all the help you can get.

I mean that you're throwing away all your chances for nothing. You think that people are what they pretend to be: that the way you were taught at school and college to think right and proper is the way things really are. But it's not: it's all only a pretence, to keep the cowardly slavish common run of people quiet. Do you want to find that out, like other women, at forty, when you've thrown yourself away and lost your chances; or won't you take it in good time now from your own mother, that loves and swears to you that it's truth: gospel truth? (*Urgently.*) Vivie: the big people, the clever people, the managing people, all know it. They do as I do, and think what I think. I know plenty of them. I know them to speak to, to introduce you to, to make friends of for you. I don't mean anything wrong: that's what you don't understand: your head is full of ignorant ideas about me. What do the people that taught you know about life or about people like me? When did they ever meet me, or speak to me, or let anyone tell them about me? the fools! Would they ever have done anything for you if I hadn't paid them? Haven't I told you that I want you to be respectable? Haven't I brought you up to be respectable? And how can you keep it up without my money and my influence and Lizzie's friends? Can't you see that you're cutting your own throat as well as breaking my heart in turning your back on me?

Much Ado about Nothing

William Shakespeare

20s

Comic

Beatrice overhears Hero and Ursala talking about Benedick and concludes that Benedick is in love with her.

What fire is in mine ears? Can this be true?
Stand I condemn'd for pride and scorn so much?
Contempt, farewell! and maiden pride, adieu!
No glory lives behind the back of such.
And, Benedick, love on; I will requite thee,
Taming my wild heart to thy loving hand:
If thou dost love, my kindness shall incite thee
To bind our loves up in a holy band;
For others say thou dost deserve, and I
Believe it better than reportingly.

Othello

William Shakespeare

20–35

Dramatic

Desdemona turns to Iago to help understand what she has done to warrant such disdain from her husband.

O good Iago,
What shall I do to win my lord again?
Good friend, go to him; for, by this light of heaven,
I know not how I lost him. Here I kneel:
If e'er my will did trespass 'gainst his love,
Either in discourse of thought or actual deed,
Or that mine eyes, mine ears, or any sense,
Delighted them in any other form;
Or that I do not yet, and ever did.
And ever will — though he do shake me off
To beggarly divorcement — love him dearly,
Comfort forswear me! Unkindness may do much;
And his unkindness may defeat my life,
But never taint my love. I cannot say "whore":
It does abhor me now I speak the word;
To do the act that might the addition earn
Not the world's mass of vanity could make me.

The Phoenician Women

Euripides

Translated by Carl R. Mueller

40–45

Dramatic

Iokaste's sons, Eteoklês and Polyneikês, agreed to rule Thebes in alternative years. She condemns their headstrong ways.

(*To Eteoklês.*) And what's this obsession with tyranny, this injustice that you praise so extravagantly? What's so remarkable about it? Is it so grand to be the object of every eye? No! An empty gain! Or is it mountains of wealth in your house you long for? But what of the troubles that accompany it? Where's the advantage? More and more and more! It's only a word! To meet life's needs is sufficient for the man with sense.

Yes, now let me ask you a question — no, two, two in one — yes. Which would you prefer? To rule, or to save Thebes? Will it be to rule, I wonder? And when — or if — Argive spears conquer Thebes? What then? Captive Theban women dragged off by the hair, forced into slavery, raped by marauding Argive warriors? This wealth of yours, that you so lust for, will have come at a high cost to Thebes! But, then — you are an ambitious man. So much for that. Now to you, Polyneikês.

The favor Adrastos did you was sheer folly, and your coming to attack this city nothing less than madness! Let's assume you do sack Thebes — which heaven forbid! — how will you celebrate the death of your own city? What trophies will you set up along the Inachos? And how inscribe them? "Having torched his city, Polyneikês dedicates these arms in honor of the gods!"? Never let this be your fame in Greece, my son! And yet, what if he overcomes you, his forces superior to yours, conquers you?

How will you return to Argos, leaving behind so many countless Argive corpses? Someone will say, some Argive: "Adrastos, what have you done? One misguided marriage, and Argos is ruined!" You're faced with two evils, my child: Fail at Thebes and you lose Argos as well.

Both of you, rein in this insanity! When two fools meet, the end is disaster!

Polly Honeycombe
George Colman

Teens
Comic

Polly, taking life's cues from novels, behaves in life as if she lived in one.

Novels, Nursee, novels! A novel is the only thing to teach a girl life, and the way of the world, and elegant fancies, and love to the end of the chapter. [. . .] Do you think, Nursee, I should have had such a good notion of love so early, if I had not read novels? [. . .] I can tell the nature of a masquerade as well as I had been at twenty. [. . .]Oh, Nursee a novel is the only thing! I tell you what, Nursee. I'll marry Mr. Scribble, and not marry Mr. Ledger, whether papa and mama choose it or no. And how do you think I'll contrive it? [. . .] I intend to elope! Yes, run away, to be sure. Why, there's nothing in that, you know. Every girl elopes, when her parents are obstinate and ill-natured about marrying her. It was just so with Betsy Thompson, and Sally Wilkins, and Clarinda, and Leonora in the History of Dick Careless, and Julia, in the Adventures of Tom Ramble and fifty others — did not they all elope? And so will I, too. I have as much right to elope as they had, for I have as much love and as much spirit as the best of them.

The Projectors

John Wilson

20s–30s

Seriocomic

Mrs. Godsgood rallies the women to stand up for themselves.

You cannot be ignorant how much your husbands have encroached upon you, or, to speak truth, how much we have all lost by letting the men engross all business to themselves, without so much as asking our advice, as if we, forsooth, were no part of them, and made to no other end but to sit at home and prick our fingers. [. . .] I have heard of an old emperor, somewhere or t'other, that ordain'd that, as he had his council of men, so his wife should have hers of women, which should be independent, and without appeal to t'other! [. . .] This council . . . whether in jest or earnest it matter not, they call'd the She Senate; and this is that which our present interest should prick us forward to restore! Nor let it be any rub in the way that women are forbid to speak in public, that being meant of a congregation of men, and I speak only of a congregation of women; for otherwise, if we were ever to hold our tongues, to what use were they give us? . . . Think you, I warrant, they were given us to no other end but to lick our teeth and cheapen eggs? I think not! And why should we not use 'em, then? [. . .] How common is it with them to be five days in wording the question, and as many more e'er they can put it right, and perhaps at last make nothing of it; whereas we are plain downright — we think what we please, and speak what we think! . . . [If] the reins were in our hands, if we did not manage them better, I am sure it could not be worse!

Prometheus Bound

Aeschylus

Translated by Carl R. Mueller

20–30

Dramatic

Io, a mortal whom Zeus loved and whom Hera, out of jealousy, has made partly cowlike in form, relates her tale to Prometheus.

Such dreams plagued me night after night,
        till one day I went to my father, and
        he sent to Delphi and Dodona
messengers to learn what word or deed
                would appease the gods.
But they brought back only riddling, muddled
                                oracles.
Then one day it came,
        an oracle,
                clear,
        to my father,
                from Apollo:
"Banish her,
banish the girl,
from your house,
from your country,
let her wander the wide Earth to its
very ends.
Refuse and Zeus' fiery thunderbolt will
dash to perdition
you, your house, and your
                                race!"

Hearing the words of Apollo,
          my father yielded,
tears in his eyes, as in mine,
          and banished me from my
                    home and country.
[. . .]
Suddenly I was changed,
          deformed,
                    my mind,
                    my body,
                    these horns,
as you see!
[. . .]

                              You have my story.
Now tell me what lies ahead,
          what sorrows will come.
Don't pity me and cover me with lies.
False words are the foulest plague.

The Provoked Wife

Sir John Vanbrugh

20s

Comic

Lady Brute provokes herself into behaving badly.

I never loved him, yet I have been ever true to him, and that in spite of all the attacks of art and nature upon poor weak women's heart in favor of a tempting love. Methinks so noble a defense as I have made should be rewarded with a better usage. Or who can tell? Perhaps a good part of what I suffer from my husband may be a judgment upon me for my cruelty to my lover. Lord, with what pleasure could I indulge that thought, were there but a possibility of finding arguments to make it good. And how do I know but there may? Let me see. What opposes? My matrimonial vow? Why, what did I vow? I think I promised to be true to my husband. Well, and he promised to be kind to me. But he hasn't kept his word. Why then, I'm absolved from mine. Aye, that seems clear to me. The argument's good between the king and the people, why not between the husband and the wife? O, but that condition was not expressed. No matter, 'twas understood. Well, by all I see, if I argue the matter a little longer with myself, I han't find so many bugbears in the way as I thought I should. Lord, what fine notions of virtue do we women take up upon the credit of old foolish philosophers. Virtue's it own reward, virtue's this, virtue's that. Virtue's an ass . . .

The Relapse

Sir John Vanbrugh

20s

Dramatic

Amanda catches her lover with a younger woman and vows revenge.

Would the world were on fire, and you in the middle on't.
Begone; leave me.
At last I am convinced. My eyes are testimonies
Of his falsehood. The base, ungrateful, perjured villain.
Good gods, what slippery stuff are men composed of?
Sure the account of their creation's false
And 'twas the woman's rib they were formed of. [. . .]
'Tis an ill cause, indeed, where nothing's to be said for't.
My beauty possibly is in the wane;
Perhaps sixteen has greater charms for him.
Yes, there's the secret. But let him know,
My quiver's not entirely emptied yet:
I still have darts and I can shoot 'em too,
They're not so blunt but they can enter still,
The want's not in my power, but in my will.
Virtue's his friend, or, through another's heart
I yet could find the way to make him smart.

The Rivals

Richard Brinsley Sheridan

40+

Comic

While expressing her disdain for educating women "too much," Mrs. Malaprop makes the case against herself by mangling the English language.

Observe me, Sir Anthony — I would by no means wish a daughter of mine to be a progeny of learning. I don't think so much leaning becomes a young woman. For instance — I would ever let her meddle with Greek or Hebrew, or Algebra or Simony, or Fluxions, or Paradoxes, or such inflammatory branches of learning; nor will it be necessary for her to handle any of your mathematical, astronomical, diabolical instruments; but, Sir Anthony, I would send her, at nine years old, to a boarding school, in order to learn a little ingenuity and artifice. Then sir, she should have supercilious knowledge in accounts; and as she grew up, I would have her instructed in geometry, that she might know something of the contagious countries. Above all, she should not mispronounce or misspell words as our young ladies of the present day constantly do. This, Sir Anthony, is what I would have a woman know; and I don't think there is a superstitious article in it.

The Roaring Girl

Thomas Dekker and Thomas Middleton

20s

Comic

Moll accosts a potential suitor for assuming she's an easy catch.

Thou'rt one of those
That thinks each woman thy fond flexible whore;
If she but cast a liberal eye upon thee,
Turn back her head, she's thine [. . .]
How many of our sex, by such as thou,
Have their good thought paid with a blasted name
That never deserved loosely, or did trip
In path of whoredom beyond cup and lip. [. . .]
What durst move you, sir,
To think me whorish? [. . .]
But why, good fisherman,
Am I thought meat for you, that never yet
Had angling rod cast towards me? 'Cause you'll say,
I'm given to sport, I'm often merry, jest,
Had mirth no kindred in the world but lust,
Oh, shame take all her friends then! But howe'er
Thou and the baser world censure my life,
I'll send 'em word by thee, and write so much
Upon thy breast, 'cause thou shalt bear in mind,
Tell them twere base to yield where I have conquered;
I scorn to prostitute myself to a man,
I that can prostitute a man to me;
And so I greet thee.

Romeo and Juliet

William Shakespeare

Teen

Dramatic

Juliet speaks from her balcony, unaware that Romeo is listening nearby.

O Romeo, Romeo! wherefore art thou Romeo?
Deny thy father and refuse thy name;
Or, if thou wilt not, be but sworn my love,
And I'll no longer be a Capulet. [. . .]
'Tis but thy name that is my enemy;
Thou art thyself, though not a Montague.
What's Montague? it is nor hand, nor foot,
Nor arm, nor face, nor any other part
Belonging to a man. O, be some other name!
What's in a name? that which we call a rose
By any other name would smell as sweet;
So Romeo would, were he not Romeo call'd,
Retain that dear perfection which he owes
Without that title. Romeo, doff thy name,
And for that name which is no part of thee
Take all myself.

The Rover

Aphra Behn

20s

Dramatic

Angellica experiences love, which becomes her undoing.

You said you loved me.
And at that instant, I gave you my heart.
I'd pride enough and love enough to think
That it could raise thy soul above the vulgar,
Nay, make you all soul, too, and soft and constant.
Why did you lie and cheapen me? Alas,
I thought all men were born to be my slaves
And wore my power like lightning in my eyes;
But when love held the mirror that cruel glass
Reflected all the weakness of my soul,
My pride was turned to a submissive passion
And so I bowed, which I ne'er did before
To anyone or anything but Heaven.
I thought that I had won you, and that you
Would value me the higher for my folly.
But now I see you gave me no more than dog lust,
Made me your spaniel-bitch; and so I fell
Like a long-worshipped idol at the last
Perceived a fraud, a cheat, a bauble. Why
Didst though destroy my too long fancied power?
Why didst thou give me oaths? Why didst thou kneel
And make me soft? Why, why, didst thou enslave me?

The Rover

Aphra Behn

20s

Dramatic

Lucetta, a galley whore and slave, empathizes with an Essex calf on board the ship.

This gold will buy us things. Alas, I curse my future that has made me a slave to Sancho, since I was sold. Would I had coin enough to fly to England and try my fortune as the colonel did. But what base means we girls o' the galleys must submit to, ere we can gain our ends. A common whore; oh fie; one that must yield to all beastly embraces, yea, all the nasty devices men's lust can invent; nay, not only obey but the fire, too, and hazard all diseases when their lust commands. And so sometimes we are enjoyed aforetimes, but never after. And yet I cannot but laugh at this English fool. If I cannot rise in this bad world, yet 'tis some recompense to bring such a fellow down. O, now is this bull calf as naked as I was once on shipboard, and now I pity him. There's for thee, poor Essex calf.

The Ruddigore, or The Witch's Curse

William Schwenk Gilbert

18–20

Seriocomic

1887, Cornwall, England. When asked by her aunt why she has yet to accept a suitor, Rose Maybud, a village maiden of discriminating taste, reveals that she lives by very strict rules of etiquette and may therefore never reveal her true feelings to a man.

Hush, dear aunt, for thy words pain me sorely. Hung in a plated dish-cover to the knocker of the work-house door, with naught that I could call mine own, save a change of baby-linen and a book of etiquette, little wonder if I have always regarded that work as a voice from a parent's tomb. This hallowed volume (*Producing a book of etiquette.*) composed, if I may believe the title-page, by no less an authority than the wife of a Lord Mayor, has been, through life, my guide and monitor. By its solemn precepts I have learnt to test the moral worth of all who approach me. The man who bites his bread, or eats peas with a knife, I look upon as a lost creature, and he who has not acquired the proper way of entering and leaving a room is the object of my pitying horror. There are those in this village who bite their nails, dear aunt, and nearly all are wont to use their pocket combs in public places. In truth I could pursue this painful theme much further, but behold, I have said enough.

The Sack of Rome

Mercy Otis Warren

20s–30s
Dramatic

As Rome falls, Edoxia resigns herself and deplores the violent nature of man.

Where shall I fly? to what sequestered shade
Where the world's distant din no more alarms,
Or warring passions burst through natures tie
And make mankind creation's a foulest stain.
Horror and guilt stare wild in every eye;
Freedom extinguished in the flames of lust
Bleeds fresh beside Rome's long expiring fame;
Virtue's become the rude barbarian's jest,
Bartered for gold, and floating down the tide
Of foreign vice, stained with domestic guilt!
Oh, could I hide in some dark hermitage
Beneath some hollow, dismal, broken cliff,
I'd weep forlorn the miseries of Rome
Till time's last hollow broke, and left me quiet
On the naked strange. Ah! Leo,
Durst thou be still the friend of sad Edoxia?
Hast thou the courage yet to visit grief,
And sooth a wretch by sympathetic tears
And reconcile me to the name of man?
Canst show me one less cruel than the tiger
Nursed in the wilds and feasting on the flesh
Of all but his own species?
This predilection's left to man alone,
To drink and riot on his brother's blood.

Saint Joan

George Bernard Shaw

Late teens
Dramatic

Joan, betrayed and accused of blasphemy, treason, and witchcraft, chooses death over imprisonment.

Light your fire: do you think I dread it as much as the life of a rat in a hole? [. . .] You think that life is nothing but not being stone dead. It is not the bread and water I fear. I can live on bread; when have I asked for more? It is no hardship to drink water if the water be clean. Bread has no sorrow for me, and water no affliction. But to shut me from the light of the sky and the sight of the fields and flowers; to chain my feet so that I can never again ride with the soldiers nor climb the hills; to make me breathe foul damp darkness, and keep from me everything that brings me back to the love of God when your wickedness and foolishness tempt me to hate Him: all this worse than the furnace in the Bible that was heated seven times. I could do without my war horse; I could drag about in a skirt; I could let the banners and the trumpets and the knights and soldiers pass me and leave me behind as they leave the other women, if only I could still hear the wind in the trees, the larks in the sunshine, the young lambs crying through the healthy frost, and the blessed, blessed church bells that send my angel voices floating to me on the wind. But without these things I cannot live; and by your wanting to take them away from me, or from any human creature, I know that your counsel is of the devil and that mine is of God.

The Seagull

Anton Chekhov

Translated by Carol Rocamora

43

Seriocomic

Treplev, a young playwright, presents his newest work to his mother, Madame Arkadina, an actress, and her friends. Madame Arkadina insists on interrupting the play with jests; Treplev stops the play and storms off, leaving Arkadina to wonder what his problem is.

What's the matter with him? [. . .]

Well, what in the world did I say to him? [. . .]

He told us beforehand it was all in fun, so that's how I took it, for fun. [. . .]

Now it appears that he's written a great masterpiece. I mean, really! Here he went and put on this show and sprayed us all with sulphur, not to entertain us, but to teach us a lesson on how to write plays and how to act on the stage. Really, it's too much. And these constant attacks against me, these diatribes, say whatever you like, I am sick and tired of them. He's a willful, egotistical little boy. [. . .]

Fine, let him write whatever he feels like writing, only spare me, please. [. . .]

(*Lights up a cigarette.*) And I'm not angry, only it irritates me to see a young man waste his time like that. I didn't mean to hurt his feelings.

The Silent Woman, or Epicoene

Ben Jonson

30+

Comic

Mistress Otter blasts her husband for letting his dogs into the house, then threatens to cut him off and take away his nice clothes.

By that light, I'll ha' you chained up with your bull-dogs and bear-dogs, if you be not civil the sooner. I'll send you to the kennel, I' faith. [. . .] Must my house, or my roof, be polluted with the scent of bears and bulls, when it is perfumed for great ladies? Is this according to the instrument when I married you? That I would be princess and reign in mine own house, and you would be my subject and obey me? What did you bring me, should make you thus peremptory? Do I allow you half-crown a day to spend where you will among your gamesters, to vex and torment me at such times as these? Who gives you your horse-mean and man's meat? Your three suits of apparel a year? Your four pair of stocking, one silk, three worsted? [. . .] Were you ever so much as looked upon by a lord, or a lady, before I married you, but on the Easter or Whitsun holidays [. . .]? Answer me to that. [. . .] Go to, behave yourself distinctly, and with good morality, or I protest, I'll take away your exhibition.

The Spanish Tragedy

Thomas Kyd

40–50

Dramatic

When Isabella is told that her beloved son, Horatio, has been murdered, she goes to the arbor where the killers hung his body and before taking her own life destroys it.

Tell me no more! — O monstrous homicides!
Since neither piety nor pity moves
The King to justice or compassion,
I will revenge myself upon this place,
Where thus they murdered my belovèd son.
(*She cuts down the arbor.*)
I will not leave a root, a stalk, a tree,
A bough, a branch, a blossom, nor a leaf,
No, not an herb within this garden plot,
Accursèd complot of my misery.
Fruitless for ever may this garden be,
Barren the earth, and blissless whosoever
Imagines not to keep it unmanured. [. . .]
And passengers, for fear to be infect,
Shall stand aloof, and, looking at it, tell:
"There, murdered, died the son of Isabel."
Ay, here he died, and here I him embrace. [. . .]
And as I curse this tree from further fruit,
So shall my womb be cursèd for his sake;
And with this weapon will I wound the breast,
The hapless breast that gave Horatio suck.
(*She stabs herself.*)

Spring's Awakening

Frank Wedekind

Translated by Carl R. Mueller

20s

Seriocomic

Ilsa speaks to her childhood friend Moritz of her Bohemian life as a model and lover of various painters.

I never get a hangover. At Carnival last year I didn't get into bed or out of my clothes for three days and nights. I just went from one party to another without stop. Henry found me the third night. [. . .] He stumbled over my arm. I was passed out in the snow. That's how I happened to move in with him. I didn't leave his house for two weeks. God, what a time that was! In the morning I had to throw on his Persian bathrobe and in the evening traipse around in a black page's costume. He must have photographed me in a million different positions, from Ganymede to a female Nebuchadnezzar on all fours. And all the while he raved on about murder, and shooting, and suicide, and coal smoke. Early every morning he brought a pistol to bed, loaded it, pointed it at my breast, and threatened to shoot. And he would, too, Moritz, he would have, too. [. . .] That bullet would have gone straight through my spine!

[. . .] In the ceiling over the bed there was a big mirror. That little room seemed tall as a tower and bright as an opera house. — You saw yourself hanging down live from the sky. Oh, and the terrible dreams I had. — God, o God, won't it ever be daylight! — Goodnight, Ilse. When you're asleep you're so beautiful I could murder you!

The Stronger

August Strindberg
Translated by Carl R. Mueller

35–45
Seriocomic

Mrs. X is a married actress; Miss Y is an unmarried actress. They meet in a café and have a "conversation" — though Miss Y never speaks.

Amelia, darling, really! Sitting here like some lonely bachelor on Christmas Eve! (*Miss Y looks up from the magazine, nods, and continues reading.*) Really, I feel sorry for you, dear, alone — alone in a café — on Christmas Eve of all times! Almost as sorry, I must say, as a wedding breakfast I once saw in a Paris restaurant — the bride sat reading a humor magazine while the groom was off playing billiards with the best man and the ushers. Goodness, I thought to myself, with such a beginning, how will it all end! Imagine, playing billiards on his wedding day! Yes, and I can just hear you about to respond: "After all, she *was* reading a humor magazine!" Yes, well, it's not quite the same, don't you see. (*A Waitress brings a cup of hot chocolate and places it in front of Mrs. X, then goes out.*) I hate to say this, Amelia, but I think you'd have done better if you'd kept your fiancé. After all, I was the first person to tell you to forgive him. But, then, how could you forget. Imagine, you'd be married now, with a home. Do you remember that Christmas in the country with your fiancé's parents, and how happy you were? How you went on and on about all that really matters is the joy of home and family life, and how you longed to get away from the theater! It's true, my darling, it is, a home is certainly the best — after the theater, of course — and then the children, you know — well, no, I suppose you wouldn't know that, would you, Amelia —

The Stronger

August Strindberg
Translated by Carl R. Mueller

35–45
Seriocomic

Mrs. X is a married actress; Miss Y is an unmarried actress. They meet in a café and have a "conversation" — though Miss Y never speaks.

Goodness, I should be ashamed of myself for making fun of my husband like this. But he's really very sweet, an absolute darling of a husband. — You really should have had one just like him, Amelia! Why, what are you laughing at? Mm? Mm? And then, well, you see, I know he's faithful to me. I know, for he's told me so himself, indeed he has. No doubt about it. Now, whatever are you grinning at? Well, for example, while I was on my Norwegian tour, that nasty little Frederique tried to seduce him. Really, now, can you imagine anything so, so, so brazen! (*Pause.*) I'd have scratched her beady little eyes clear out of her head if she'd come around while I was at home! (*Pause.*) It was a good thing he told me himself. Imagine hearing it from some gossip! (*Pause.*) Frederique, of course, wasn't the only one. Oh, I just don't know why, but women go absolutely crazy over my husband. They all seem to want him. They must think he has some influence at the theater because he's in the government. Who knows, perhaps even you may have had your claws out for him. I've never quite trusted you, you know. But now, of course, I know that he was never really interested in you. And then there was always that grudge you seemed to hold against him. (*Pause. They look at each other with a kind of edgy uncertainty.*) All right, now, Amelia, look, I want you to come spend the evening with us, just to show you're not mad at us, at least not at me. I really find it terribly unpleasant being on bad terms with people — especially you. Perhaps it was because I got that part that you were so terribly set on — (*Gradually more slowly.*) — or — oh, I don't know — not the foggiest, really, you know — (*Pause.*)

The Summer People

Maxim Gorky

Translated by Nicholas Saunders and Frank Dwyer

60

Dramatic

Ogla, the Russian equivalent of a drama queen, resents the life she leads and lashes out at her generous friend, Varvara.

I hate myself because I'm so helpless without you . . . yes, hate myself! . . . You think it's easy for me to take your money? . . . How can I have any respect for myself when I'm such a failure at everything? . . . when I have to have somebody else helping me and supporting me my whole life long . . . You know something? Sometimes I don't even like you very much! . . . In fact, I hate you! . . . Because you're so composed and logical and you never really let yourself go, and you don't seem to have any feelings . . . Those who help others secretly despise them, I know that . . . I want to be one of the helpers. [. . .] I don't like people! I don't like Marya Lvovna — why is she always judging everyone? I don't like Ryumin — he talks and talks, but he never dares and he never does. I don't like your husband, either — he's gotten soft as dough, and he's afraid of you . . . is that what you want? [. . .] I want to live! I'm as good as anybody else! I'm not stupid, I see everything . . . I see that you yourself, for example . . . oh, yes, I see everything! . . . you have a good life. Your husband has plenty of money . . . he's not particularly scrupulous in his business dealings, your husband . . . everybody knows that. Well, you must know it yourself! . . . and you, too . . . you've managed to arrange things so as not to have any children . . . [. . .] Forgive me . . . please forgive me. I don't know what makes me this way . . .

The Summer People

Maxim Gorky

Translated by Nicholas Saunders and Frank Dwyer

20s

Dramatic

In this passionate speech, Marya Lvovna begs her discontented friends and family to use their privileged station in life to lift others from poverty.

Oh, my friends, this is no way for us to live! We're the children of washerwomen and cooks — strong, healthy people of the working-class and we should not be living this way! Don't you see, in all our country's history, there has never been a generation like ours, educated people with the blood of ordinary men and women in their veins . . . So our very blood should inspire us to improve, and enlighten, and renew the lives of those dear ones, who spend all their days working, choking in the mud and darkness, gasping for air . . . We must devote ourselves to improving their lives, not out of pity or charity . . . but for our own sake . . . so that we don't feel so isolated, so that we can avoid looking down from our lofty heights into the abyss that opens before us, and separates us from our brothers below, who live by the sweat of their brows and look up at us as at enemies! Surely we were sent ahead to find a path for them, a path that will lead them to a better life . . . but instead, we have abandoned them, we have lost our way, and we have created this terrible loneliness in which we are divided against ourselves, in which all we can do is scurry about frantically, in increasing desperation . . . That's our tragedy! And we have done this to ourselves, we deserve our misery! It's true, Varya, we have no right to fill the air with our groans.

Three Weeks after Marriage

Samuel Foote

40+

Comic

Blind to her own abusive behavior, Lady Racket condemns another woman while speaking to her husband.

[. . .] You aren't fit to be about my person. I might as well not be married, for any use you are of. Reach me a chair. You have no compassion for me. I am so glad to sit down! Why do you drag me to routs? You know I hate them. I'm out of humor. I lost all my money. I hate gaming. It almost metamorphoses a woman into fury. Do you know that I was frighted at myself several times tonight? I had a huge oath at the very tip of my tongue. [. . .] I caught myself at it, but I bet my lips and so I did not disgrace myself. And then I was crammed up in a corner of the room with such a strange party at a whist table, looking at black and red spots. Did you mind them? There was that strange, unaccountable woman, Mrs. Nightshade. She behaves so strangely to her husband, a poor, inoffensive good natured, good sort of a good for nothing kind of man, but she so teased him — "How could you play that card? Ah, you have a head and so has a pin! You are a numskull, you know are — Madam, he has the poorest head in the world, he does not know what he is about — you know you don't — Ah, fie! I am ashamed of you." Why don't you hand me upstairs? Oh, I am so tired. [. . .] You awkward thing, let me alone!

Titus Andronicus

William Shakespeare

40s

Dramatic

Tamora, captive queen of the Goths, now married to the Roman emperor, Titus. When Titus Andronicus sacrifices one of her sons to appease the spirits of the members of his family slain in the war with the Goths, Tamora vows revenge. During a royal hunt, Tamora slips away with Aaron, her beloved Moorish attendant, to plot her redress. When the two are discovered by Lavinia and her husband, Bassanius, the former accuses Tamora of adultery against the emperor with Aaron. Calling for her two remaining sons, Tamora tells the following lie, which she hopes will clear her of any adulterous charge while inciting the boys to murder Bassinius.

Have I not reason, think you, to look pale?
These two have 'ticed me hither to this place:
A barren detested vale, you see it is;
The trees, though summer, yet forlorn and lean,
O'ercome with moss and baleful mistletoe:
Here never shines the sun; here nothing breeds,
Unless the nightly owl or fatal raven:
And when they show'd me this abhorred pit,
They told me, here, at dead time of the night,
A thousand fiends, a thousand hissing snakes,
Ten thousand swelling toads, as many urchins,
Would make such fearful and confused cries
As any mortal body hearing it
Should straight fall mad, or else die suddenly.
No sooner had they told this hellish tale,

But straight they told me they would bind me here
Unto the body of a dismal yew,
And leave me to this miserable death:
And then they call'd me foul adultress,
Lascivious Goth, and all the bitterest terms
That ever ear did hear to such effect:
And, had you not by wondrous fortune come,
This vengeance on me had they executed.
Revenge it, as you love your mother's life,
Or be ye not henceforth call'd my children.

Titus Andronicus

William Shakespeare

40s

Dramatic

Tamora pleads for her sons' lives.

Stay, Roman brethren! Gracious conqueror,
Victorious Titus, rue the tears I shed,
A mother's tears in passion for her son:
And if thy sons were ever dear to thee,
O, think my son to be as dear to me!
Sufficeth not that we are brought to Rome,
To beautify thy triumphs and return,
Captive to thee and to thy Roman yoke,
But must my sons be slaughter'd in the streets,
For valiant doings in their country's cause?
O, if to fight for king and commonweal
Were piety in thine, it is in these.
Andronicus, stain not thy tomb with blood:
Wilt thou draw near the nature of the gods?
Draw near them then in being merciful:
Sweet mercy is nobility's true badge:
Thrice noble Titus, spare my first-born son.

Titus Andronicus

William Shakespeare

40s

Dramatic

Tamora, in her attempt to drive Titus mad, disguises herself as Revenge.

Know, thou sad man, I am not Tamora;
She is thy enemy, and I thy friend:
I am Revenge: sent from the infernal kingdom,
To ease the gnawing vulture of thy mind,
By working wreakful vengeance on thy foes.
Come down, and welcome me to this world's light;
Confer with me of murder and of death:
There's not a hollow cave or lurking-place,
No vast obscurity or misty vale,
Where bloody murder or detested rape
Can couch for fear, but I will find them out;
And in their ears tell them my dreadful name,
Revenge, which makes the foul offender quake.

The Trojan Women

Euripides

Translated by Carl R. Mueller

35–45

Dramatic

Over the body of the sacrificed boy, Astyanax, Hekabe laments the decline of her homeland, Troy.

(*Speaks as if in a trance.*) Now, now it is revealed, now — the gods don't care, the gods don't hear, the gods are nothing and all that matters is pain, my pain and Troy's, Troy of all cities most hated by the gods. It was for nothing, the sacrificing, the hecatombs, the oxen, all in vain, their smoke never reached the heavens. And yet had the god not crushed our city, not turned our world on its head, deep, deep in the dark earth, we had been nothing, we had faded into oblivion, unknown in obscurity, never the subject of song sung by the Muses in
time to come.

Go bury the boy now in his wretched grave. He has all the adornments that are due the underworld. What difference can it make to the dead how lavish the funeral. This is an empty pretension of the living.

The Trojan Women

Euripides

Translated by Carl R. Mueller

35–45

Dramatic

Andromachê begs for the life of her young son, Astyanax.

Greeks! You call yourselves Greeks but contrive atrocities worthy of barbarians! Why are you killing this child? What has he done to you? And you, Helen, you, daughter of Tyndareos, never a daughter of Zeus! It was many fathers fathered you! Vindictiveness, Hate, Slaughter, Death, and all the wickedness the earth breeds! Zeus was never your father, that much I know, for you were born a plague to Greeks and barbarians alike! I curse you! You whose ravishing eyes brought ugly death to the glorious plains of Troy!

So, come, then, Greeks, come take him, take him and toss him, hurl him to his death, if that satisfies your will! Feast on his flesh! We're pawns in the gods' game, and they're destroying me who cannot save my child from death. Cover me, my wretched body, and fling me onto your ship! What a splendid marriage I go to across the death of my child.

The Two Gentlemen of Verona

William Shakespeare

16–20

Seriocomic

Julia, a young woman in love, has received a love letter from Proteus and in a fit of pique tears it up before having read it. Here, the impetuous young woman gathers all the scraps and tries to piece the letter back together again.

O hateful hands, to tear such loving words!
Injurious wasps, to feed on such sweet honey
And kill the bees that yield it with your stings!
I'll kiss each several paper for amends.
Look, here is writ "kind Julia." Unkind Julia!
As in revenge of thy ingratitude,
I throw thy name against the bruising stones,
Trampling contemptuously on thy disdain.
And here is writ "love-wounded Proteus."
Poor wounded name! my bosom as a bed
Shall lodge thee till thy wound be thoroughly heal'd;
And thus I search it with a sovereign kiss.
But twice or thrice was "Proteus" written down.
Be calm, good wind, blow not a word away
Till I have found each letter in the letter,
Except mine own name: that some whirlwind bear
Unto a ragged fearful-hanging rock
And throw it thence into the raging sea!
Lo, here in one line is his name twice writ,
"Poor forlorn Proteus, passionate Proteus,
To the sweet Julia:" that I'll tear away.

And yet I will not, sith so prettily
He couples it to his complaining names.
Thus will I fold them one upon another:
Now kiss, embrace, contend, do what you will.

Uncle Vanya

Anton Chekhov

Translated by Carol Rocamora

24

Dramatic

Sonya attempts to rescue Uncle Vanya, who is crumbling under the heavy burdens of his life.

What can we do, we must live! (*Pause.*)

We shall live, Uncle Vanya. We shall live through the endless, endless row of days, the long evenings, we shall patiently bear the ordeals that fate has in store for us; we shall toil for others now and in our old age, we shall know no rest, and when our hour comes, we shall die humbly, and there beyond the grave we shall say that we've suffered, that we've wept, that life was bitter, and God will take pity on us, and you and I, uncle, darling uncle, we shall see a radiant life, a beautiful, blissful life, we shall rejoice, and we shall look back on our present unhappiness with tenderness, with a smile — and we shall rest. I believe it, Uncle Vanya, I believe it fervently, passionately . . . (*Gets on her knees before him and puts her head in his hands; in a tired voice.*) We shall rest!

Vera, or The Nihilists

Oscar Wilde

20s

Dramatic

1880, Moscow. When the czar declares martial law, Vera, the outspoken daughter of an innkeeper, speaks passionately in favor of revolution.

Martial law! O God, how easy it is for a king to kill his people by thousands, but we cannot rid ourselves of one crowned man in Europe! What is there of awful majesty in these men which makes the hand unsteady, the dagger treacherous, the pistol-shot harmless? Are they not men of like passions with ourselves, vulnerable to the same diseases, of flesh and blood not different from our own? What made Olgiati tremble at the supreme crisis of that Roman life, and Guido's nerve fail him when he should have been of iron and of steel? A plague, I say, on these fools of Naples, Berlin, and Spain! Methinks that if I stood face to face with one of the crowned men my eye would see more clearly, my aim be more sure, my whole body gain a strength and power that was not my own! Oh, to think what stands between us and freedom in Europe! a few old men wrinkled, feeble, tottering dotards whom a boy could strangle for a ducat, or a woman stab in a night-time. And these are the things that keep us from democracy, that keep us from liberty. But now methinks the brood of men is dead and the dull earth grown sick of childbearing, else would no crowned dog pollute God's air by living.

The Way of the World
William Congreve

20s
Comic

Millament agrees to marry Mirabell, under these conditions . . .

Good Mirabell, don't let us be familiar or fond, nor kiss before folks [. . .] Let us never visit together, nor go to a play together, But let us be very strange and well bred: let us be as strange as if we had been married a great while; and as well bred as if we were not married at all. [. . .] Liberty to pay and receive visits to and from whom I please, to write and receive Letters, without interrogatories or wry faces on your part. To wear what I please; and choose conversations only to my own taste; to have no obligation upon me to converse with wits that I don't like, because they are your acquaintance; or to be intimate with fools, because they may be your relations. Come to dinner when I please, dine in my dressing room when I'm out of humor without giving a reason. To have my closet inviolate; to be sole-empress of my tea-table, which you must never presume to approach without first asking leave. And lastly, where ever I am, you shall always knock at the door before you come in. These Articles subscrib'd, if I continue to endure you a little longer, I may by degrees dwindle into a Wife.

The Way to Keep Him
Arthur Murphy

20s
Comic

Muslin complains about men, love, and marriage.

What the deuce is here to do? Shall I go and fix my heart upon a man, that shall despise me for that very reason, and, "Ay," says he, "poor fool, I see she loves me — the woman's well enough, only she has one inconvenient circumstance about her: I'm married to her, and marriage is the Devil." — And then when he's going a-roguing, smiles impudently in your face, and, "M dear, divert yourself, I'm just going to kill half an hour at the chocolate-house, or to peep in at the play; your servant, my dear, your servant." — fie upon 'em! I know 'em all. — Give me a husband that will enlarge the circle of my innocent pleasures: but a husband nowadays, Ma'am, is no such a thing. — A husband — the Devil take'em all — Lord forgive one for swearing — is nothing at all but a bug-bear, a snapdragon; a husband, Ma'am is a mere monster; that is to say, if one makes him so; then, for certain, he is a monster indeed; and if one does not make him so, then behaves like a monster, and of the two evils, by my troth — Ma'am, was you ever at the play of Catherine and Mercutio? The vile man calls his wife his goods, and his cattles, and his household stuff. — There you may see, Ma'am, what a husband is —

The Wild Duck

Henrik Ibsen
Translated by Rick Davis and
Brian Johnston

Teens
Dramatic

Her father has just discovered that Hedwig is not, in fact, his daughter. Hedwig suspects the truth when his love for her — and the wild duck that they nurture — takes an ugly turn.

Daddy! Daddy! Don't go away from me. He'll never come back to us again. I think I'm going to die of all this. What have I done to him? Mother, why doesn't Daddy want to see me any more? I think I know what it is. Perhaps I'm not Daddy's real child. And now perhaps he has found it out. I've read about that sort of thing. But I think he might be just as fond of me for all that. Almost more. The wild duck was sent us as a present too, and I'm tremendously fond of that, just the same. The poor wild duck! He can't bear to look at that any more, either. Just think he wanted to wring its neck. I say a prayer for the wild duck every night and ask that it shall be protected from death and everything bad. I taught myself to say my prayers because there was a time when Daddy was ill and had leeches on his neck and said he was lying at death's door. So I said a prayer for him when I'd gone to bed. And I've gone on with it ever since. I thought I'd better put in the wild duck too, because she was so delicate at first. And now you say I should sacrifice the wild duck to prove my love for Daddy. I will try it. I will ask Grandfather to shoot the wild duck for me.

The Witch of Edmonton

William Rowley, Thomas Dekker, and John Ford

50–70
Dramatic

Elizabeth Sawyer, believed by all to be a witch, here reveals her desire to live up to everyone's expectations so that she may wreak revenge on those who have abused her.

Still vexed! Still tortured! That curmudgeon Banks
Is ground of all my scandal. I am shunned
And hated like a sickness, made a scorn
To all degrees and sexes. I have heard old beldams
Talk of familiars in the shape of mice,
Rats, ferrets, weasels and I wot not what,
That have appeared and sucked, some say, their blood.
But by what means they came acquainted with them
I'm now ignorant. Would some power, good or bad,
Instruct me which way I might be revenged
Upon this churl, I'd go out of myself
And give this fury leave to dwell within
This ruined cottage ready to fall with age,
Abjure all goodness, be at hate with prayer,
And study curses, imprecations,
Blasphemous speeches, oaths, detested oaths,
Or anything that's ill; so I might work
Revenge upon this miser, this black cur
That barks and bites, and sucks the very blood
Of me and of my credit. 'Tis all one
To be a witch as to be counted one.
Vengeance, shame, ruin light upon that canker!

The Witch of Edmonton

William Rowley, Thomas Dekker, and John Ford

50–70
Dramatic

Elizabeth Sawyer has been sent a doglike familiar from the dark lord she has promised to serve. The familiar has committed much mischief at her bequest and has become very dear to the old witch. Here, she calls for her satanic familiar.

Still wronged by every slave, and not a dog
Bark in his dame's defence? I am called witch,
Yet am myself bewitched from doing harm.
Have I given up myself to thy black lust
Thus to be scorned? Not see me in three days!
I'm lost without my Tomalin. Prithee come.
Revenge to me is sweeter far than life;
Thou art my raven on whose coal-black wings
Revenge comes flying to me. O my best love!
I am on fire, even in the midst of ice,
Raking my blood up till my shrunk knees feel
Thy curled head leaning on them. Come then, my darling.
If in the air thou hover'st, fall upon me
In some dark cloud; and as I oft have seen
Dragons and serpents in the elements,
Appear thou now so to me. Art thou i'th' sea?
Muster up all the monsters from the deep,
And be the ugliest of them. So that my bulch
Show but his swart cheek to me, let earth cleave
And break from hell, I care not! Could I run
Like a swift powder-mine beneath the world,

Up would I blow it all to find out thee,
Though I lay ruined in it. Not yet come!
I must then fall to my old prayer,
Sanctibiceter nomen tuum.

A Woman Killed with Kindness

Thomas Heywood

30s

Dramatic

England. Anne has been lured into an unfortunate dalliance by the unscrupulous Wendoll, a supposed friend of her husband's. When the affair is found out, she tearfully abases herself in front of her husband.

I would I had no tongue, no ears, no eyes,
No apprehension, no capacity.
When do you spurn me like a dog? When tread me
Under your feet? When drag me by the hair?
Though I deserve a thousand thousand fold
More than you can inflict, yet, once my husband,
For womanhood — to which I am a shame
Though once an ornament — even for His sake
That hath redeem'd our souls, mark not my face
Nor hack me with your sword, but let me go
Perfect and undeformed to my tomb!
I am not worthy that I should prevail
In the least suit, not to speak to you,
Nor look on you, nor to be in your presence;
Yet as an abject this one suit I crave,
This granted I am ready for my grave.

A Woman of No Importance

Oscar Wilde

30s

Comic

Mrs. Allonby has specific ideas about what constitutes the Ideal Man.

The Ideal Man! Oh, the Ideal Man should talk to us as if we were goddesses, and treat us as if we were children. He should refuse all our serious requests, and gratify every one of our whims. He should encourage us to have caprices, and forbid us to have missions. He should always say much more than he means, and always mean much more than he says. [. . .] If we ask him a question about anything, he should give us an answer all about ourselves. He should invariably praise us for whatever qualities he knows we haven't got. But he should be pitiless, quite pitiless, in reproaching us for the virtues that we have never dreamed of possessing. He should never believe that we know the use of useful things. That would be unforgivable. But he should shower on us everything we don't want. He should persistently compromise us in public, and treat us with absolute respect when we are alone. And yet he should be always ready to have a perfectly terrible scene, whenever we want one, and to become miserable, absolutely miserable, at a moment's notice, and to overwhelm us with just reproaches in less than twenty minutes, and to be positively violent at the end of half an hour, and to leave us for ever at a quarter to eight, when we have to go and dress for dinner. And when, after that, one has seen him for really the last time, and he has refused to take back the little things he has given one, and promised never to communicate with one again, or to write one any foolish letters, he should be perfectly broken-hearted, and telegraph to one all day long, and send one little notes every half-hour by a private hansom, and dine quite alone at the club, so that every one should know how unhappy he was.

The Women of Trachis

Sophokles

Translated by Carl R. Mueller and Anna Krajewska-Wieczorek

30s

Dramatic

To win back her husband's love, Deianeira used a charm given to her by a mystical beast. But the charm went horribly wrong, and Deianeira accidentally tortured and killed Herakles instead. Here, the Nurse tells of Deianeira's fate.

She went into the house — went in alone —
And anything she touched that once she'd used,
Some domestic piece, or, rushing through the house,
Saw a much-loved servant, she would cry,
Poor creature, howl at her fate and the fate
Of her house, that they would have no more children.
Then stopping suddenly, she rushes into his room,
The room that she had shared with Herakles,
And unseen by her, I watch from a hidden place.
She makes his bed, her husband's bed, casting
Coverings over it, and then leaps into its middle
And dissolves in a flood of hot tears, saying:
"Dear bed, dear bed of love, goodbye forever!
You'll never again hold me as a wife!"
She was quiet then. But all at once,
With a violent sweep, she tears open her robe,
Held at her breast by a golden brooch, baring
Her whole left side and arm.
As fast as I could,

I ran to tell her son of what she planned,
But time ran out, and when we returned she'd thrust
A two-edged sword deep in her side and heart.
[. . .]
That's how things are inside this house.
Only a fool counts on the future
Before we've passed today unharmed!

The Women of Trachis

Sophokles
Translated by Carl R. Mueller and
Anna Krajewska-Wieczorek

30s
Dramatic

Deianeira, wife of Herakles, learns her husband went to war over love for another woman. Adding insult to injury, Herakles has sent the girl ahead, to share Deianeira's bed. Here, she declares herself ready to win back her husband.

This is my reward
For all the weary years I've guarded his home,
Herakles,
Whom I called true and loyal, my honest love!
Angry? How can I be angry?
He's suffered the same disease often enough.
But to live in one house, we two together,
Wife and mistress, to share one marriage?
What woman could countenance that?
Her flower
Is coming to bloom, mine fading. Men's eyes
Adore plucking a youthful blossom,
But turn away when it withers.
What do I fear, then?
That I will call him husband,
But she will share his bed.
She's the younger. But as I've said: anger
Is not for the wife; not a wife of good judgment. [. . .]

I am no friend to evil,
Nor do I care to know or learn anything of it.
I detest women who do.
And yet, if there is some charm, some spell to use
On Herakles, to regain his love, to defeat
This girl, then I am ready.

MALE MONOLOGUES

Aias

Sophokles
Translated by Carl R. Mueller and
Anna Krajewska-Wieczorekk

30s
Dramatic

On the eve of his death, Aias calls for his son.

Son, your father's life has not been lucky;
Be luckier than he was. But in all else
Be your father's equal and you'll be no coward.
And yet what is there I wouldn't give
To be where you are now:
Ignorant of the evil that surrounds you.
Life is sweetest when innocence is yours,
Before you know the meaning of joy and sorrow.
But once you know, then prove to your father's enemies
The man you are and the man your father was.
Till then, let light breezes nourish you,
And enjoy your young life, your mother's joy.
You may be sure no Greek will ever outrage
Or shame you, even when I am gone. [. . .]

But now, son, take this broadshield with your name:
Eurysakes — seven layers thick
Of hardened oxhide; proof against any spear;
Hold it, wield it, here, by the well-stitched strap.
The rest of my armor will share my grave.
(*To Tekmessa.*)
Take him. Here. Quickly!
Take him away!

Aias

Sophokles

Translated by Carl R. Mueller and Anna Krajewska-Wieczorekk

30s

Dramatic

Aias, determined to kill himself, is crouched down, planting the haft of his sword in the earth so that he may plunge himself onto it.

There —
The sacrificial slayer ready —
Just at the angle to be most cutting.
But why all the talk — less thinking —

The sword was Hektor's. A gift from him.
The man of all men that I most hated.
And there it stands.
Planted in enemy Trojan soil.
Edge new-whetted by the iron-scouring stone.
Buried with care for a kind and easy death.
There. Ready. Everything in order.
Now for my prayers.

Almighty Zeus,
I call first on you, as is only right:
Give me your protection.
I ask one small favor.

Alkestis

Euripides

Translated by Carl R. Mueller

30s

Dramatic

Herakles, drunk, crowned with myrtle, and carrying a wineskin and cup, addresses a servant, who is sad over the death of Alkestis.

Hey! You! Come here! Why so grim, friend? So much worry! Servants ought to be cheerful to a guest, not all the time scowling. I mean, I mean, here I am, oldest friend your master's got, and you mope around, your forehead wrinkled like a prune, all in a tizzy over somebody dying who wasn't even part of the family. Come over here, let me tell you something. What do you know about the human condition? Aha! Just as I thought! Nothing! Well! How could you? We all have to die. That's the dirty little secret. That's it! And, sad to say, we never know if today's our last. And what a pity. Not to know where you're headed, and nothing you can do about it. Zilch! So now you know, cheer up, you hear? One day at a time! Wet your whistle! Bend the elbow! Bottoms up! It's yours, the whole day! And all the rest is Fortune's.

André

William Dunlop

40s

Dramatic

The village of Tappan, New York, during the Revolutionary War. Melville, captain in the Colonial army, is standing the night watch at an encampment outside Tappan. He takes a moment to reflect on the dark nature of war.

The solemn hour, "when night and morning meet."
Mysterious time, to superstition dear,
And superstition's guides, now passes by;
Deathlike in solitude. The sentinels,
In drowsy tones, from post to post send on
The signal of the passing hour. "All's well,"
Sounds through the camp. Alas, all is not well;
Else, why stand I, as man, the friend of man,
At midnight's depth, deck'd in this murderous guise,
The habiliment of death, the badge of dire
Necessitous coercion. 'Tis not well.
— In vain the enlighten'd friends of suffering man
Point out, of war, the folly, guilt, and madness.
Still, age succeeds to age, and war to war;
And man, the murderer, marshals out in hosts
In all gaiety of festive pomp,
To spread around him death and desolation.
How long! how long! —
— Methinks I hear the tread of feet this way.
My meditating mood may work me woe.
(*Draws.*) Stand, whoso'er thou art. Answer.
Who's there?

André

William Dunlop

20–30
Dramatic

On the last night of his life Major André, a convicted British spy, contemplates his impending death.

Kind Heaven be thank'd for that I stand alone
In this sad hour of life's brief pilgrimage!
Single in misery; no one else involving.
In grief, in shame, and ruin. 'Tis my comfort.
Thou, my thrice honor'd sire, in peace went'st down
Unto the tomb, nor knew to blush, not knew
A pang for me. And thou, revered matron,
Could'st bless thy child, and yield thy breath in peace!
No wife shall weep, no child lament my loss.
Thus may I consolation find in what
Was once my woe. I little thought to joy
In not possessing, as I erst possest,
thy love, Honora! André's death, perhaps,
May cause a cloud pass o'er thy lovely face;
The pearly tear may steal from either eye;
For thou mayest feel a transient pang, nor wrong
A husband's rights: more than a transient pang
O mayest thou never feel! The morn draws nigh
To light me to my shame. Frail nature shrinks —
And is death then so fearful? I have brav'd
Him, fearless, in the field, and steel'd my breast
Against his thousand horrors; but his cool,
His sure approach, requires a fortitude
Which naught but conscious rectitude can give.

Antigone

Sophokles

Translated by Carl R. Mueller and Anna Krajewska-Wieczorek

Teens–20s

Dramatic

For burying her brother, Antigone has been condemned to death by her uncle, Kreon, King of Thebes. Here, Kreon's son, Haimon, begs his father to reconsider his verdict.

[Father,] [. . .] I hear what they're saying, I hear their whispers,
Their muttered words in the dark,
And how they mourn the girl.
They say no woman ever deserved a fate
So evil; that no one ever died so dishonored

A death for an act so glorious.
"What's so terrible?" they ask.
"She only covered her slaughtered brother's body,
A body, naked, lying in the field,
Unburied, because she couldn't bear to see it
Torn to shreds, mangled by dogs and vultures.
A brother killed in battle! Where's the offense?
She deserves a golden prize, not our scorn!"
[. . .]
Father, I beg of you, don't make the mistake of thinking
That only you are right. The man who thinks so,
The man who believes that only he has wisdom,
That he alone has the gift of words, the power
Of Reason — that man, when you lay him open,
Is seen to be empty. There's no shame in yielding
To Reason, even for a wise man.

Antony and Cleopatra

William Shakespeare

35–45

Dramatic

Antony accepts that he has been betrayed.

All is lost;
This foul Egyptian hath betrayed me:
My fleet hath yielded to the foe; and yonder
They cast their caps up and carouse together
Like friends long lost. Triple-turn'd whore!
'tis thou
Hast sold me to this novice; and my heart
Makes only wars on thee. Bid them all fly;
For when I am revenged upon my charm,
I have done all. Bid them all fly; begone.
(*Exit Scarus.*)
O sun, thy uprise shall I see no more:
Fortune and Antony part here; even here
Do we shake hands. All come to this? The hearts
That spaniel'd me at heels, to whom I gave
Their wishes, do discandy, melt their sweets
On blossoming Caesar; and this pine is bark'd,
That overtopp'd them all. Betray'd I am:
O this false soul of Egypt! this grave charm, —
Whose eye beck'd forth my wars, and call'd them home;
Whose bosom was my crownet, my chief end, —
Like a right gipsy, hath, at fast and loose,
Beguiled me to the very heart of loss.
What, Eros, Eros!

Arms and the Man

George Bernard Shaw

30–40

Seriocomic

Bulgaria. Nicola takes his position in the Petkoff household very seriously. When Louka, a peasant-girl-turned-chambermaid, behaves in a manner he believes to be above her station, he lectures her on the importance of knowing one's place.

You have a great ambition in you, Louka. Remember: if any luck comes to you, it was I that made a woman of you. [. . .]

Yes, me. Who was it made you give up wearing a couple of pounds of false black hair on your head and reddening your lips and cheeks like any other Bulgarian girl? I did. Who taught you to trim your nails, and keep your hands clean, and be dainty about yourself, like a fine Russian lady? Me: do you hear that? me! (*She tosses her head defiantly; and he turns away, adding, more coolly.*) [. . .]

[J]ust listen to my advice. If you want to be a lady, your present behavior to me won't do at all, unless when we're alone. It's too sharp and impudent; and impudence is a sort of familiarity: it shews affection for me. And don't you try being high and mighty with me, either. You're like all country girls: you think it's genteel to treat a servant the way I treat a stableboy. That's only your ignorance; and don't you forget it. And don't be so ready to defy everybody. Act as if you expected to have your own way, not as if you expected to be ordered about. The way to get on as a lady is the same as the way to get on as a servant: you've got to know your place: that's the secret of it. And you may depend on me to know my place if you get promoted. Think over it my girl. I'll stand by you; one servant should always stand by another.

The Bakkhai

Euripides

Translated by Carl R. Mueller

50+

Dramatic

When the young Pentheus chastises the old seer Teiresias for taking part in the festive Bakkhic rituals, Teiresias defends his devotion to Dionysos.

Give a wise man an honest case to argue and words come easy. But *your* words, young man, the words that fall easy from *your* tongue, are neither wise *nor* clever. A man whose strength rests solely in his self-assurance is a bad citizen. For all his words, he's short on reason. He's a fool.

This new god you ridicule? There are no words for how great his fame will be throughout all Hellas.

[. . .]

Listen to me, Pentheus. Don't mistake that force alone governs human affairs. And if your mind is sick, don't presume to think yourself sane. Welcome this god to Thebes. Pour out wine in his honor. Wreathe your head with garlands and dance the Bakkhic dance.

As for that matter that causes you so much torment: sex. Oh my boy, Dionysos doesn't suppress lust in a woman. You must look for that in the woman herself, in her nature. Not even at the height of Bakkhic ecstasy will a chaste woman be anything less than chaste. Just think, my boy, the pleasure you take when throngs stand at the gates, magnifying the name of Pentheus.

Gods, no less than kings, demand respect. And so, Kadmos and I, for all your scoffing, your insane laughter, will wreathe our heads with ivy, take up our wands, and old and gray as we are, we will dance the god's dance. Two old fools, no doubt, but dance we will, for we have no choice. No logic of yours will persuade me to fight the god. For you are mad, Pentheus, cruelly mad, and no drug can cure your sickness, though a drug must surely have caused it.

The Bear

Anton Chekhov

Translated by Carol Rocamora

35–50

Comic

Grigory Stepanovich Smirnov, a landowner, has come to collect a debt from the ever-grieving widow, Popova, who tells him she is "not in the mood" to deal with financial matters today.

(*Alone.*) Well, excu-u-use me! Not in the mood . . . Her husband died seven months ago! And what about me? Do I have to pay my interest or don't I? I ask you: Do I or don't I? All right, your husband died, you're not in the mood, whatever . . . your steward's gone off somewhere, curse him, so what am I supposed to do? Flee from my creditors in an hot air balloon? Take a flying leap and bash my head against a wall? I go and call on Gruzdev — and nobody's home. Yaroshevich is in hiding. I have a knock-down-drag-out fight with Kuritzyn and almost hurl him out a window, Mazutov has cholera, and this one is "not in the mood." Not one of these swine will pay me. And all because I've spoiled them, I'm a "Milquetoast," a sniveler, a soft touch! I'm too easy on them! But just you wait! You will remember me! I will not be trifled with, confound it! I'll stand my ground — I'll stay here until she pays up, that's what I'll do! Brrrr! . . . I'm in a rage today, a real rage! I'm shaking with fury, I can't even breathe . . . My God, I feel positively faint!

The Bear

Anton Chekhov

Translated by Carol Rocamora

35–50

Comic

Grigory Stepanovich Smirnov, a landowner, has come to collect a debt from the ever-grieving widow, Popova, who tells him his manner is coarse and that he does not know how to conduct himself around women.

I mean, this is amazing! How do you expect me to talk to you? In French, or what? (*Fuming, he lisps.*) Madame, je vous prie . . . how happy I am that you haven't paid me my money yet . . . Oh, pardon, I've disturbed you! Lovely weather we're having today! And how charming you look all in black! (*Bows and scrapes.*)

[. . .] And I don't know how to conduct myself in female company! My dear lady, I have seen more women in my time than you've seen sparrows! Three duels I have fought over women, I've spurned a dozen women, nine more have spurned me! Yes, indeed! Oh, there were times when I played the fool, when I whispered sweet nothings, uttered honeyed words, showered pearls of flattery, when I simpered and swooned . . . I loved, I suffered, I sighed at the moon, I pined, languished, wasted away, I blew hot and cold . . . I loved madly, passionately, every which way, heaven help me, I chattered like a magpie about emancipation, I squandered half my soul on the tender passion, and now, thank you very much, but no thank you! You beguile me no longer! Enough! [. . .] Present company excluded, of course, but all other women, great and small, they're hypocrites, phonies, gossips, scandalmongers, haters, slanderers, liars to the marrow of their bones, they're petty, fussy, ruthless, they're absolutely illogical, and as for what they've got upstairs, (*strikes his forehead*) well, forgive me for saying so, but a sparrow could outdo a philosopher if the philosopher's wearing a skirt!

The Beaver Coat

Gerhart Hauptmann

Translated by Ludwig Lewisohn

20+

Comic

Mitteldorf is not sure what's up, but is certain there's trouble brewing.

He's writin' pages an' pages! An' them must be important things, I c'n tell you that. (*Confidentially.*) An' lemme tell you: there's somethin' in the air — I ain't sayin' I know exactly what. But there's somethin' — I know that as sure's . . . You just look out, that's all, and you'll live to see it. It's goin' to come down — somethin' — and when it do — look out. That's all I say. No, I don't pretend to understand them things. It's all new doin's to me. That's what they calls modern. An' I don't know nothin' about that. But somethin's got to happen. Things can't go on this way. The whole place is got to be cleaned out. I can't say 's I gets the hang of it. I'm too old. But talk about the justice what died. Why, he wasn't nothin' but a dam' fool to this one. I could go an' tell you all kinds o' things, but I ain't got no time. The baron'll be missin' me. (*He goes, but having arrived at the door, turns back.*) The lightnin' is goin' to strike, Mrs. Wolff. Take my word for that!

Before Dawn

Gerhart Hauptmann

Translated by Ludwig Lewisohn

30+

Dramatic

Hoffmann, an engineer, fears that an upstart will blow the whistle on working conditions.

I must tell you that I consider your appearance and demeanor here — to put it mildly — incredibly impudent. You come here, enjoy my hospitality, thresh out a few of your thread-bare phrases, turn my sister-in-law's head, go on about old friendships and other pleasant things, and then you tell me quite coolly: you're going to write a descriptive pamphlet about the local conditions. Why, what do you take me to be, anyhow? D'you suppose I don't know that these so-called essays are merely shameless libels? . . . You want to write a denunciation like that, and about our coal district, of all places! Are you so blind that you can't see whom such a rag would harm most keenly? Only me, of course! I tell you, the trade that you demagogues drive ought to be more firmly stamped out than has been done up to now! What is it you do? You make the miners discontent, presumptuous; you stir them up, embitter them, make them rebellious, disobedient, wretched! Then you delude them with promises of mountains of gold, and, in the meantime, grab out of their pockets the few pennies that keep them from starving! You ridiculous, pompous wind-bag! Go to work! Leave off this silly driveling! Do something!

The Beggar's Opera

John Gay

30s

Seriocomic

1728, London. The infamous Macheath, a notorious highwayman, greets the strumpets he has summoned to his lair for an evening's entertainment.

Dear Mrs. Coaxer, you are welcome. You look charmingly today. I hope you don't want the repairs of quality, and lay on paint. — Dolly Trull! kiss me, you slut; are you as amorous as ever, hussy? You are always so taken up with stealing hearts, that you don't allow yourself time to steal anything else. — Ah, Dolly, thou wilt ever be a coquette. — [. . .] — Betty Doxy! Come hither, hussy. Do you drink as hard as ever? You had better stick to good wholesome beer; for in troth, Betty, strong waters will in time ruin your constitution. You should leave those to your betters. — What! and my pretty Jenny Diver too! As prim and demure as ever! There is not any prude, though ever so high bred, hath a more sanctified look, with a more mischievous heart. Ah! thou art a dear artful hypocrite. — Mrs. Slammekin! as careless and genteel as ever! all you fine ladies, who know your own beauty, affect an undress. — But see, here's Suky Tawdry come to contradict what I was saying. Everything she gets one way, she lays out upon her back. Why, Suky, you must keep at least a dozen tally-men. — [. . .] But hark! I hear music. The harper is at the door. "If music be the food of love, play on." Ere you seat yourselves, ladies, what think you of a dance! —

Black-ey'd Susan

Douglas Jerrold

30s

Dramatic

After many months at sea, William finally returns home, his thoughts on one person only: his lovely wife, Susan.

Avast there! hang it — that name, spoke by another, has brought the salt water up; I can feel one tear standing in either eye like a marine at each gangway: but come, let's send them below. (*Wipes his eyes.*) Now, don't pay away your line till I pipe. I have been three years at sea; all that time I heard but once from Susan — she has been to me a main-stay in all weathers. I have been piped up — roused from my hammock, dreaming of her — for the cold black middle watch; I have walked the deck, the surf beating in my face, but Susan was at my side, and I did not feel it; I have been reefing on the yards, in cold and darkness, when I could hardly see the hand of my next messmate — but Susan's eyes were on me, and there was light; I have heard the boatswain pipe to quarters — a voice in my heart whispered "Susan!" it was a word that seemed to turn the balls aside, and keep me safe. When land was cried from the mast head, I seized the glass — my shipmates saw the cliffs of England — I, I could see but Susan! I leap upon the beach; my shipmates find hands to grasp and lips to press — I find not Susan's.

The Blunderer

Molière

Translated by Henri van Laun

20+

Comic

Mascarille informs his friend that his infatuation with a certain young woman has not gone unnoticed.

Your love is like porridge, which by too fierce a fire swells, mounts up to the brim, and runs over everywhere! Everybody might have seen it. At table, when Trufaldin made her sit down, you never took your eyes off her, blushed, looked quite silly, cast sheep's eyes at her, without ever minding what you were helped to; you were never thirsty but when she drank, and took the glass eagerly from her hands; and without rinsing it, or throwing a drop if it away, you drank what she left in it, and seemed to choose in preference that side of the glass which her lips had touched; upon every piece which her slender hand had touched, or which she had bit, you laid your paw as quickly as a cat does upon a mouse, and you swallowed it as glibly as if you were a regular glutton. Then, besides all this, you made an intolerable noise, shuffling with your feet under the table, for which Trufaldin, who received two lusty kicks, twice punished a couple of innocent dogs, who would have growled at you if they dared; and yet, in spite of all this, you say you have behaved finely! For my part I sat upon thorns all the time; notwithstanding the cold, I feel even now in a perspiration. I hung over you just as a bowler does over his ball after he has thrown it, and thought to restrain your actions by contorting my body ever so many times!

The Confederacy

Sir John Vanbrugh

30–40s

Seriocomic

1705, London. Brass and Dick are a couple of nefarious ne'er-do-wells who have scrambled from one scheme to the next with Dick always coming out on top of things. Here, Brass finally objects to always playing second fiddle.

In short, look smooth, and be a good Prince, I am your Valet, 'tis true: Your Footman sometimes, which I enrag'd at; but you have always had the ascendant, I confess; when we were School-fellows, you made me carry your Books, make your Exercise, own your Rogueries, and sometimes take a Whipping for you: When we were Fellow-Prentices, tho' I was your Senior, you made me open the Shop, clean my Master's shoes, cut last at Dinner, and eat all the Crust. In our sins too, I must own you still kept me under; you soar'd up to Adultery with our Mistress, while I was at humble Fornication with the Maid. Nay, in our Punishments, you still made good your Post; for when once upon a time I was sentenced but to be Whip'd, I cannot deny but you were condemn'd to be Hang'd. So that in all times, I must confess, your Inclinations have been greater and nobler than mine. However, I cannot consent that you shou'd at once fix Fortune for Life, and I dwell in my Humilities for the rest of my Days.

Cyrano de Bergerac

Edmond Rostand

Translated by Charles Marowitz

40+

Seriocomic

When his rival, Valvert, boldly asserts that Cyrano's nose is "rather large," Cyrano responds with an impressive, poetic salvo.

But my dear fellow,
That will not do at all. There is so much
To say on such a topic, I can't believe
You'd throw away the chance. — You might begin
Par exemple, aggressively: "Were that
My nose, I'd have it surgically removed!"
Or Amiably: "How can you drink with such
A monstrous protuberance? Why I'd
Forego the mug and simply use a barrel!"
Descriptively: "Why it's a rock, a crag,
A promont'ry; an archipelago!"
Inquisitively: "I say, is it some kind of
Carrying-case for a trombone or a tuba?"
Courteously: "Do you adore the birds
So much that when the robins come to roost
You give them that to perch on?"
[. . .]
These, my friend, are things you might have said
Had you had some sprinklings of wit
To spice your tedious discourse.

Cyrano de Bergerac

Edmond Rostand

Translated by Charles Marowitz

40+

Dramatic

Cyrano bravely reveals to his friend the fear that his will be a loveless existence.

O look me in the face
Dear friend. What kind of chance have I
With this protuberance between my eyes?
I have no illusions. — Even though
I must admit I sometimes fantasize,
Walking in the evening through the bower
With the raindrops drying on the leaves,
Inhaling April's fragrance through these nostrils;
Watching lovers strolling arm in arm
And yearning for a woman of my own
To fondle gently underneath the moon,
Bantering and trading tender phrases.
I lose myself within this reverie
Until I glimpse the shadow of my profile
Mocking me upon the garden-wall.
[. . .]
(*Drooping.*)
I have my hours of desolation
Knowing myself so ugly and alone [. . .]

Danton's Death

George Büchner

Translated by Henry J. Schmidt

40–50

Dramatic

Paris. The sardonic Camille bemoans the fact that art generally goes unappreciated by the masses.

I tell you, if they aren't given everything in wooden copies, scattered about in theaters, concerts, and art exhibits, they'll have neither eyes nor ears for it. Let someone whittle a marionette where the strings pulling it are plainly visible and whose joints crack at every step in iambic pentameter: what a character, what consistency! Let someone take a little bit of feeling, an aphorism, a concept, and clothe it in a coat and pants, give it hands and feet, color its face and let the thing torment itself through three acts until it finally marries or shoots itself: an idea! Let someone fiddle an opera which reflects the rising and sinking of the human spirit the way a clay pipe with water imitates a nightingale: oh, art!

Take people out of the theater and put them in the street: oh, miserable reality! They forget their Creator because of His poor imitators. They see and hear nothing of Creation, which renews itself every moment in and around them, glowing, rushing, luminous. They go to the theater, read poetry and novels, make faces like the masks they find there, and say to God's creatures: how ordinary! The Greeks knew what they were saying when they declared that Pygmalion's statue did indeed come to life but never had any children.

Darnley

Edward Bulwer-Lytton

30–40

Dramatic

London. When Darnley's wife requests that they separate, Darnley takes a moment to verbally vent his frustration with the fairer sex.

Oh! let man beware of marriage until he thoroughly know the mind of her on whom his future must depend. Woe to him, agony and woe, when the wife feels no sympathy with the toil, when she soothes not in the struggle, when her heart is far from that world within, to which her breath gives the life, and her presence is the sun! How many men in humbler life have fled, from a cheerless hearth, to the haunts of guilt! How many in the convict's exile, in the felon's cell, might have shunned the fall — if woman (whom Heaven meant for our better angel) had allured their step from the first paths to hell by making a paradise of home! But by the poor the holy household ties are at least not scorned and trifled with, as by those among whom you were reared. *They* at least do not deem it a mean ambition that contents itself with the duties of wife and mother. Look round the gay world you live in, and when you see the faithless husband wasting health, fortune, honor, in unseemly vices — behold too often the cause of all in the cold eyes and barren heart of the fashionable wife.

Doctor Faustus

Christopher Marlowe

35+

Dramatic

Faustus, at the end of his damned life.

Ah, Faustus.
Now hast thou but one bare hour to live,
And then thou must be damn'd perpetually!
Stand still, you ever-moving spheres of heaven,
That time may cease, and midnight never come;
Fair Nature's eye, rise, rise again, and make
Perpetual day; or let this hour be but
A year, a month, a week, a natural day,
That Faustus may repent and save his soul!
O lente, lente currite, noctis equi!
The stars move still, time runs, the clock will strike,
The devil will come, and Faustus must be damn'd.
O, I'll leap up to my God! — Who pulls me down? —
See, see, where Christ's blood streams in the firmament!
One drop would save my soul, half a drop: ah, my Christ! —
Ah, rend not my heart for naming of my Christ!
Yet will I call on him: O, spare me, Lucifer! —
Where is it now? tis gone: and see, where God
Stretcheth out his arm, and bends his ireful brows!
Mountains and hills, come, come, and fall on me,
And hide me from the heavy wrath of God!
No, no!

A Doll House

Henrik Ibsen

Translated by Rick Davis and Brian Johnston

25–30s

Dramatic

Helmer condescendingly forgives his wife, Nora, for a money scheme she concocted behind his back.

Try to calm down, collect your thoughts, my little, shivering songbird. If you need protection, I have broad wings to shelter you with. (*Walks around near the door.*) Oh, Nora — our home is so snug, so cozy. This is your nest, where I can keep you like a dove that I've snatched, unharmed, from the falcon's claws; I'll bring peace and rest to your beating heart. Little by little it will happen, Nora, believe me. Tomorrow, this will all seem different to you; and soon everything will be back to normal. I won't need to keep saying I forgive you — you'll feel it, you'll know it's true. How could you ever think I could bring myself to disown you, or even punish you? You don't know how a man's heart works, Nora. There's something indescribably sweet and satisfying for a man in knowing he's forgiven his wife — forgiven her from the bottom of his heart. It's as if he possesses her doubly now — as if she were born into the world all over again — and she becomes, in a way, his wife and his child at the same time. And that's what you'll be for me from now on, you little, helpless, confused creature. Don't be frightened of anything — just open your heart to me and I'll be both your conscience and your will.

An Enemy of the People

Henrik Ibsen

Translated by Rick Davis and Brian Johnston

30s–40s

Dramatic

Dr. Stockmann's discovery of a public health threat turns his hometown against him. A mob pelts his home with rocks.

Isn't that extraordinary — this revolting cowardice! Here, let me show you something! See, here are all the stones they pelted us with. But look at them! I swear, not more than two decent fighting rocks in the whole heap — the others are just pebbles — bits of gravel! And yet they stood out there howling and swearing they were going to batter me into oblivion. But action — action — no, you don't see much of that in this town. [. . .] — because if the time comes for a serious fight — say, to defend the country — you'll see, Captain Horster, how public opinion will take to its heels; you'll witness the solid majority rushing into the woods like a flock of sheep. That's what so painful to think about, that's what hurts so much. No, what the hell — this is all so stupid. They've called me an enemy of the people, and an enemy of the people I'll be. [. . .] An ugly word can work like a pin-prick in the lung. And that damn word, I can't get rid of it — it's lodged itself here below my heart, and it lies there and stings and burns like acid. And nothing will cure it!

The Father

August Strindberg

Translated by Carl R. Mueller

35+

Dramatic

The Captain and his wife are fighting over the future of their child. The wife has been spreading rumors about the Captain's mental stability. Here, he confronts her with an ultimatum.

[. . .] I gather from these letters that you have for some time been working to turn all of my former friends against me by spreading rumors regarding my mental condition. And your efforts have been rewarded, for no one from the commanding officer down to the cook believes me to be sane. As for the facts concerning my illness, they are these. My capacity to reason, as you are aware, is unaffected, and so I am fit to fulfill my duties both as a military man and as a father. As for my emotions, they are more or less under my control, and will remain so as long as my willpower continues relatively intact. You, however, have gnawed and gnawed at it so vehemently that the worn cogs will soon slip their wheel and the entire mechanism fly out of control. I don't intend to appeal to your feelings, since you have none — and that is your strength — but I will appeal to your self-interest. [. . .]

Your behavior has succeeded in rousing my suspicions to where my judgment is blunted and my thoughts have begun to wander — the very event you've waited for — my approaching insanity that can arrive at any moment. You are now faced with the question: Is it more to your interest that I be of sound or unsound mind. Think about it! If I collapse, I lose my job, and you will find yourself in a very awkward position. If I die, you get my insurance. If, however, I kill myself, you get nothing. Logic suggests that you have more to gain if I live out my life.

Faust

Johann Wolfgang von Goethe
Translated by Carl R. Mueller

45+
Dramatic

A narrow, high-vaulted gothic chamber. At his desk, Faust sits restlessly in his armchair.

Here I stand!

A fool!

I who have studied and crammed Philosophy,
Law, and Medicine, and even, oh, God! Theology,
from end to bitter end!
And what has it got me?

Nothing.

Not one jot wiser than before.

Oh, I have my degrees,
they call me Master of Arts, and Doctor!
And for these ten years now
I've led my students around by the nose,
upstairs, downstairs, backwards, forwards —
and learned?
That there's nothing to be learned.
Nothing!
And that is the dread that eats at my heart's core. [. . .]

And what has it got me?

Just this!
I'm a pauper.
Or nearly so.
I have neither property nor wealth,
nor worldly honor.

No glory.

Show me a dog who would lead such a life!

Gammer Gurton's Needle

William Stevenson

30–50

Seriocomic

England. Diccon, a licensed beggar newly released from Bedlam, arrives at the home of Gammer Gurton and finds all in an uproar due to the loss of the lady's sewing needle.

Many a mile have I walked, divers and sundry ways,
and many a good man's house have I been at in my days,
Many a gossip's cup in my time have I tasted,
And many a broach and spit have I both turned and basted,
Many a piece of bacon have I had out of their balks
In running over the country with long and weare walks;
Yet came my foot never within those doorcheeks,
To seek flesh, or fish, garlic, onions, or leeks,
That ever I saw a sort in such a plight
As here within this house appeareth to my sight!
There is howling and scowling, all cast in a dump,
With whewling and puling, as though they had lost a trump;
Sighing and sobbing they weep and they wail,
I marvel in my mind what the devil they ail.
The old trot sits groaning, with "alas!" and "alas!"
And Tib wrings her hands, and takes on in worse case.
With poor Cock, their boy, they be driven in such fits
I fear me the folks be not well in their wits.
Ask them what they ail, or who brought them in this stay,
They answer not at all but "alack!" and "welaway!"

Ghosts

Henrik Ibsen

Translated by Rick Davis and Brian Johnston

25–30

Dramatic

Sickly Osvald, having returned to his mother's home after many years abroad, asks for her help with an impossible task.

Mother, didn't you say that you'd do anything for me, anything in the world, if I asked you? Do you stand by that? [. . .] All right. Now you'll hear it. Mother, you have a strong mind, I know you can take this in — so now you must sit calmly while you hear what it is. And don't scream. You hear me? Promise me that? We'll sit and talk about it quietly. Promise me that, Mother? [. . .]

The illness I received as my inheritance — (*Points to his forehead.*) It sits right here. [. . .] Yes, Mother, it sits right here, lurking, ready to break out any day, any time. [. . .] I had one attack down there, it didn't last long. But when I found out what had happened to me, this dread began pursuing me, relentlessly, and so I started back home to you as fast as I could. I'm not afraid of dying, even though I'd like to live as long as I can. But this is beyond disgusting. To be turned into a helpless child again — to have to be fed, to have to be — it's unspeakable! [. . .] The doctor said it wouldn't necessarily be fatal right away. He called it a kind of softening of the brain, or something like that. (*Smiles sadly.*) I think that sounds so charming — it always make me think of red velvet curtains — something soft and delicate to stroke. (*Takes a little box from his inside breast pocket.*) See this, Mother? Morphine powder. I've managed to save twelve capsules. [. . .] So — now you have to give me that helping hand, Mother.

The Great Divide

William Vaughn Moody

30s

Dramatic

Ghent saved Ruth from a group of toughs in a frontier town by purchasing her from them. A simple man, Ghent assumed that she was his to keep. Some nine months later, they have a child. Ruth is finally able to make her way back home to Massachusetts, where she lives in shame with her family. Ghent has followed, and here eloquently pleads his love for her and their child.

(*Ruth utters a faint moan as her head sinks in her arms on the table. With trembling hands, Ghent caresses her hair lightly and speaks between a laugh and a sob.*) Little mother! Little mother! What does the past matter, when we've got the future — and him? (*Ruth does not move. He remains bending over her for some moments, then straightens up, with a gesture of stoic despair.*)

I know what you're saying there to yourself, and I guess you're right. Wrong is wrong, from the moment it happens till the crack of doom, and all the angels in heaven, working overtime, can't make it less of different by a hair. That seems to be the law. I've learned it hard, but I guess I've learned it. I've seen it written in mountain letters across the continent of this life. — Done is done, and lost is lost, and smashed to hell is smashed to hell. We fuss and potter and patch up. You might as well try to batter down the Rocky Mountains with a rabbit's heartbeat! (He goes to the door, where he turns.) You've fought hard for me, God bless you for it. — But it's been a losing game with you from the first! — You belong here, and I belong out yonder — beyond the Rockies, beyond — the Great Divide!

The Great Galeoto

José Echegaray

30s

Seriocomic

As he struggles for words, Ernest, a frustrated playwright, agonizes over writer's block.

(*Seated at table and preparing to write.*) Nothing — impossible! It is striving with the impossible. The idea is there; my head is fevered with it; I feel it. At moments an inward light illuminates it, and I see it. I see it in its floating form, vaguely outlined, and suddenly a secret voice seems to animate it, and I hear sounds of sorrow, sonorous sighs, shouts of sardonic laughter . . . a whole world of passions alive and struggling. . . . They burst forth from me, extend around me, and the air is full of them. then, then I say to myself: "Now is the moment." I take up my pen, stare into space, listen attentively, restraining my very heart-beats, and bend over the paper. . . . Ah, the irony of impotency! The outlines become blurred, the vision fades, the cries and sighs faint away . . . and nothingness, nothingness encircles me . . . the monotony of empty space, of inert thought, of idle pen and lifeless paper that lacks the life of thought! Ah! How varied are the shapes of nothingness, and how, in its dark and silent way, it mocks creatures of my stamp!

The Green Cockatoo

Arthur Schnitzler

Translated by Carl R. Mueller

40s

Dramatic

The men at The Green Cockatoo drink and talk about their wives. Here, Henri is called upon to tell the tragic story of his unfaithful wife.

(*Who has long been sunk in thought.*) Do you know my wife? She's the most beautiful and the most depraved creature alive. And I love her. We've known each other for seven years. But only yesterday she became my wife. In these seven years there wasn't a single day, not one, that she didn't lie to me. Everything about her lies. Her eyes. Her lips. Her kisses. Her smiles. She was had by every old man and every young man. By anyone who attracted her. By anyone who paid for her. And I knew it. And yet she loved me, my friends. Can you understand that? Any of you? She would come back to me. Time after time. From wherever she was. From whoever she was with. From the handsome. From the ugly. The clever. The stupid. From the tramp and the gentleman. Came back to me. Always. [. . .] I walked her to the theater. Tonight was to be the last time. I kissed her. At the door. She went up to her dressing room. And I took off like a man who hadn't a trouble in the world. But after I'd walked only a hundred yards, it began. Inside me. Do you understand? A terrible restlessness. [. . .] And I went back. Her scene was over by now. She has little to do. Stand on stage half-naked for a while and she's done. I stood in front of her dressing room door. I heard whispering. I couldn't make it out. Then it stopped. I pushed open the door. (*He screams like a wild animal.*) It was the Duke de Cadignan! I killed him!

Hamlet

William Shakespeare

25–35

Dramatic

Hamlet advises the Players.

Speak the speech, I pray you, as I pronounc'd it to you, trippingly on the tongue, but if you mouth it, as many of our players do, I had as lief the town-crier spoke my lines. Nor do not saw the air too much with your hand, thus, but use all gently, for in the very torrent, tempest, and, as I may say, whirlwind of your passion, you must acquire and beget a temperance that may give it smoothness. Oh it offends me to the soul to hear a robustious periwig-pated fellow tear a passion to totters, to very rags, to spleet the ears of the groundlings, who for the most part are capable of nothing but inexplicable dumb-shows and noise. I would have such a fellow whipt for o'erdoing Termagant, it out-herods Herod, pray you avoid it.

Hernani

Victor Hugo

Translated by Mrs. Newton Crosland

20–30

Dramatic

Hernani, a bandit, vows to revenge himself against the treacherous Don Carlos.

One of thy followers! I am, oh King!
Well said. For night and day and step by step
I follow thee, with eye upon thy path
And dagger in my hand. My race in me
Pursues thy race in thee. And now behold
Thou art my rival! For an instant I
'Twixt love and hate was balanced in the scale.
Not large enough my heart for her and thee;
In loving her oblivious I became
Of all my hate of thee. But since 'tis thou
That comes to will I should remember it,
I recollect. My love it is that tilts
Th' uncertain balance, while it falls entire
Upon the side of hate. Thy follower!
'Tis thou hast said it. [. . .] Go where
Thou wilt, I'm there to listen and to spy,
And noiselessly my step will press on thine.
No day, shouldst thou but turn thy head, oh King,
But thou wilt find me, motionless and grave,
At festivals; at night, should'st thou look back,
Still wilt thou see my flaming eyes behind.

Hernani

Victor Hugo

Translated by Mrs. Newton Crosland

20–30

Dramatic

Hernani, the infamous outlaw, pleads with Dona Sol to forsake the love that they share.

Marry the old duke then, for he is good
And noble. By the mother's side he has
Olmédo, by his father's Alcala.
With him be rich and happy by one act.
Know you not what this generous hand of mine
Can offer thee of splendour? Ah, alone
A dowry of misfortune, and the choice
Of blood or tears. Exile, captivity
And death, and terrors that environ me.
These are thy necklaces and jewelled crown.
Never elated bridegroom to his bride
Offered a casket filled more lavishly,
But 'tis with misery and mournfulness.
Marry the old man — he deserves thee well! [. . .]
To vengeance and to love I bid adieu!
My life is ending; useless I will go,
And take away with me my double dream,
Ashamed I could not punish, nor could charm.
I have been made for hate, who only wished
To love. Forgive and fly me, these my prayers
Reject them not, since they will be my last.
Thou livest — I am dead. I see not why
Thou should'st immure thee in my tomb.

Hindle Wakes

Stanley Houghton

30s

Dramatic

Alan Jeffcote, a mill-owner's son, tries to explain to Beatrice (whom he is keen on) why he spent a scandalous weekend with Fanny Hawthorn.

Of course I knew her before Blackpool. There's not so many pretty girls in Hindle that you can miss one like Fanny Hawthorn. I knew her well enough, but on the straight, mind you. I'd hardly spoken to her before I ran into her at the Tower in Blackpool. We'd just had dinner at the Metropole Grill-room, George and I, and I daresay had drunk about as much champagne as was good for us. We looked in at the Tower for a lark, and we ran into Fanny in the Ballroom. [. . .] What else do you want me to tell you?

Yes, Bee, I suppose I did think about you. But you weren't there, you see, and she was. That was what did it. Being near her and looking at her lips. Then I forgot everything else. Oh, I know. I'm a beast. I couldn't help it. I suppose you can never understand. It's too much for you to see the difference. Fanny was just an amusement - a lark. I thought of her as a girl to have a bit of fun with. Going off with her was like going off and getting tight for once in a way. You wouldn't care for me to do that, but if I did you wouldn't think very seriously about it. You wouldn't want to break off our engagement for that. I wonder if you can look on this affair of Fanny's as something like getting tight - only worse. I'm ashamed of myself, just as I should be if you caught me drunk. I can't defend myself.

Hippolytus

Euripides

Translated by Carl R. Mueller

20s

Dramatic

Hippolytus, upon being told that Phaidra, his father's wife, is in love with him, curses the fair sex in general.

Why, Zeus, why? Why did you have to make women? Why saddle mankind with this evil? This, this counterfeit coin that you call woman, fair on the outside, rotten at the core! Why? If to propagate the race, then from the start you might have provided us another means. Men should have gone to your temples to buy their progeny, paid in bronze or iron or heavy gold, each man what he can, then to go home to live in peace in houses free of women!

Woman's evil cannot be more clear. The father that gave her life and reared her up, that same father, when it comes time, puts a price on her head called a dowry, a bribe meant to induce another man to relieve him of her, and so be rid of his misery! And then there's the man, the husband, who receives this plague into his house, and rejoices in decking out his destructive idol in every finery, every jewel, until he's finally drained his house to the dregs of its wealth. Marriage to a nonentity is bound to be easiest. But even a stupid woman brings harm into the house. It's the clever ones I most abhor. May my house never hold a woman with more wits than a woman needs.

Hippolytus

Euripides

Translated by Carl R. Mueller

Teens–20s

Dramatic

Phaidra, under a spell, fell madly in love with her stepson, Hippolytus. Unable to live with the shame, she has killed herself. When her husband discovers her body, he accuses his son of having a hand in her death. Here, Hippolytus defends himself.

Father, there is one practice that I have neither touched nor been touched by; the same practice that you are so certain you have convicted me of: sex — an experience I have never shared. I know it only from talk I've overheard, and paintings, and even these I'm not intent on; my aim in life is to be pure and untainted. But it's obvious my chastity doesn't impress you. So much for that. In which case, it is for you to show me the manner of my corruption.

[. . .] I swear by Zeus Keeper of Oaths, and by the earth that supports us, that I have never touched your wife, that I have never wanted to, and that the thought could never have entered my mind. If I'm guilty in this matter, may I then be expunged from the face of creation together with my name and reputation, and may neither earth nor sea receive my polluted flesh. What terror made this woman take her life, I do not know; nor have I the freedom to say more. Though she could not be virtuous in her life, she acted virtuously; while I, who had it, used it badly.

Ivanov

Anton Chekhov
Translated by Carol Rocamora

35–45
Dramatic

Ivanov is going through a midlife crisis and feels guilt about his feelings for his terminally ill wife, Anyuta. He tries to explain himself to a friend, Lvov.

It's true, it's true . . . I'm terribly guilty, no doubt, but my head is in such confusion, such a lethargy weighs upon on my soul, and I haven't the strength even to understand myself. I understand neither myself, nor others . . . (*Glances toward the window.*) They can hear us, come . . . (*They stand.*) My dear friend, I'd tell you everything from the very beginning, but it's such a long and complicated story, that I'd be telling it till dawn. (*They walk together.*) Anyuta is a rare and wonderful woman . . . Because of me she has renounced her faith, her father and mother, her inheritance, and were I to request one hundred sacrifices more, she would perform them without blinking an eye. As for me, I am neither remarkable, nor have I sacrificed a thing. However, it's a long story . . . The fact of the matter is, dear doctor (*Considers for a moment.*), that . . . to put it succinctly, I married for passionate love, I vowed love eternal, but . . . five years have passed, she still loves me, while I . . . (*Spreads his hands in a gesture of helplessness.*) Here you've told me that she soon will die, and I feel neither love, nor regret, but rather a kind of emptiness, a weariness. To look upon me must be horrifying; and I myself don't understand what will become of my soul . . .

Joaquin Murieta de Castillo, the Celebrated California Bandit

Charles E. B. Howe

30–50

Dramatic

When his life is spared by young Joaquin, Garcia impulsively vows to never harm his savior. When Joaquin subsequently rescues a band of pioneers that Garcia had threatened to rob and kill, the bandit rages privately.

Joaquin has dared to interfere between the wolf and its victims. Hell's curse! That I should hold that oath so binding, when to cut his throat would release me from all promises. What is one life? Have I not taken twenty — aye, fifty — better, far better than his; and for less gold than old Gonzalles offered? To say I will kill Joaquin is easier said than done. I have seen him asleep close by my side, as unconscious as if he were in no danger; yet it seemed to me that whenever I approached him, with that thought on my mind, he would move uneasily in his sleep, and his eyes would open, as if his very eyes and ears did nothing but spy my acts and learn the fall of my footsteps. I hate him! No; I do not love him; then by hell and its furies, I fear him. A boy! caramba!

Joaquin Murieta de Castillo, the Celebrated California Bandit

Charles E. B. Howe

30–50

Dramatic

Garcia, a ruthless bandit and murderer, reflects on his upbringing and the reason he turned bad.

I once had a master. Hell! how my blood boils! That master was my father; my mother his slave, and I born his peon. How I have seen that man whip my mother. Large scars showed their hideousness all over her once beautiful face. She said she was once beautiful — and I believe her. That master whipped my mother once too often. It was in a by-place; I heard the lash falling on the back of one begging for mercy; I hurried to the spot — it was my mother, bleeding at every blow; I felled the hound of hell to the earth — my master, my father — I plucked his eyes out; and then he begged for what he had refused to give, Mercy. I cut limb from limb of his body; his heart I trampled under my feet. I was blood — all I saw was blood. And then my mother embraced me and called me her child — (*Laughs.*) — and I became a fiend. When I think of that first act, I could drink blood. The Past — the awful Past — I cannot think of it! What a hell is conscience!

John Gabriel Borkman

Henrik Ibsen

Translated by Rick Davis and Brian Johnston

40s

Dramatic

1896. Borkman, a former bank president, hints at the circumstances surrounding his demise.

Do you know what I maintain is the most hideous crime a man can commit? Not murder. Not robbery. Not burglary in the middle of the night. Not even perjury. These are mostly committed against people you hate — or don't care about at all. (*With emphasis.*) The most hideous crime of all is to abuse a friend's trust. [. . .] No — I'm telling you: the most hideous crime a man can commit is to reveal a friend's confidential correspondence — laying bare, for all the world to see, what was meant for one person only — in private — like a whisper in a dark, empty, locked room. A man who is capable of stooping to such means is infected — poisoned all through his being — the morality of a master criminal. I had a friend like that. And he crushed me. There wasn't one detail of my business that I didn't share with him freely. And then, at the crucial moment, he turned against me the very weapons I'd placed in his hands. [. . .] I might as well tell you, Vilhelm. It was — something to do with a woman. [. . .] Well, well, well — let's not say another word about these stupid old stories.

Judith

Friedrich Hebbel

Translated by Marion W. Sonnenfeld

40s

Dramatic

Holofernes, the tyrant of Babylon, is a violent and evil man. Here, the dreaded general of Nebuchadnezzer muses on the importance of keeping himself a mystery to his underlings.

(*Alone.*) That's the real art: not to let yourself be calculated, but always to stay a mystery. Water does not know this, so they've dammed the sea and dug a bed for the river. Fire hasn't mastered the art either; it's fallen so low that the kitchen boys have investigated its nature and now it has to boil cabbage for any rascal who wants it. Not even the sun knows it: they've spied out its path and shoemakers and tailors measure time by its shadows. But I have mastered the art! They lurk about me and peer into the cracks and crevices of my soul, and, out of every word I utter, they try to forge a wrench to open up the chambers of my heart. But my present is never consistent with my past; I am not one of those fools who fall flat on their faces in cowardly vanity and make each day the other's fool; no, I cheerfully hack up today's Holofernes into little pieces and feed him to tomorrow's Holofernes. I don't see merely a dull feeding process in life, but rather a steady transformation and rebirth of existence. [. . .] Nebuchadnezzar is, unfortunately, nothing but an arrogant cipher who passes time by eternally multiplying himself.

Judith

Friedrich Hebbel

Translated by Marion W. Sonnenfeld

40s

Dramatic

The general finds himself attracted to Judith, a captured Jew who is secretly plotting to kill him. Here, the self-centered man contemplates his assured victory over Judith, while especially relishing the thought of driving the God she loves from her heart.

A woman is a woman, and still, one imagines there is a difference. Of course, a man feels his worth more when embracing a woman than anywhere else. Ha! When, in conflict between their sensual pleasure and chastity, they tremble as they anticipate the man's embrace! When they look as though they wanted to flee, and then, suddenly overcome by their nature, they throw their arms around his neck, when their last bit of independence and self-assurance rises up and spurs them, unable to resist any longer, to cooperate willingly. If then their desire, aroused in every drop of their blood by treacherous kisses, begins to race against the man's, so that they invite where they should be resisting — yes, that is life — then one finds out why the gods took the trouble to create man; there's a satisfaction, an overflowing measure of it! [. . .] This Judith too — to be sure, her eyes look kind, and her cheeks smile like sunshine; but no one but her God dwells in her heart, and I'd like to drive him out now. When I was a young man and encountered an enemy, I'd sometimes wrestle with him until I had his sword and would then slay him with it instead of drawing my own. That's how I'd like to slay her. She's to dissolve before me because of her own feeling, because of the faithlessness of her senses!

King John

William Shakespeare

Teens

Dramatic

Arthur, the young imprisoned nephew of wicked King John, pleads with his keeper not to follow his uncle's orders — to put out his eyes.

Must you with hot irons burn out both mine eyes?
And will you?
Have you the heart? When your head did but ache
I knit my handkercher about your brows,
The best I had, a princess wrought it me,
And I did never ask it you again;
And with my hand at midnight held your head,
And like the watchful minutes to the hour,
Still and anon cheer'd up the heavy time,
Saying "What lack you?" and "Where lies your grief?"
Or "What good love may I perform for you?"
Many a poor man's son would have lain still
And ne'er have spoke a loving word to you;
But you, at your sick service, had a prince.
Nay, you may think my love was crafty love
And call it cunning: do, an if you will,
If heaven be pleas'd that you must use me ill,
Why then you must. Will you put out mine eyes?
These eyes that never did nor never shall
So much as frown on you?

The Lady of Lyons

Edward Bulwer-Lytton

20s

Seriocomic

Melnotte is a simple country boy who has fallen in love with the daughter of a wealthy merchant. When his mother chides him for courting a woman above his station, he assures her that he is more than capable of achieving his goal.

Do the stars think of us? Yet if the prisoner see them shine into his dungeon, wouldst thou bid him turn away from *their* lustre? Even so from this low cell, poverty, I lift my eyes to Pauline and forget my chains. — (*Goes to the picture and draws aside the curtain.*) See, this is her image — painted from memory. Oh, how the canvas wrongs her! — (*Takes up the brush and throws it aside.*) I shall never be a painter! I can paint no likeness but one, and that is above all art. [. . .] What is the hour? — so late? I will tell thee a secret, mother. Thou knowest that for the last six weeks I have sent every day the rarest flowers to Pauline? — she wears them. I have seen them on her breast. Ah, and then the whole universe seemed filled with odors! I have now grown more bold — I have poured my worship into poetry — I have sent the verses to Pauline — I have signed them with my own name. My messenger ought to be back by this time. I bade him wait for the answer. [. . .] She will admit me. I shall hear her speak — I shall meet her eyes — I shall read upon her cheek the swept thoughts that translate themselves into blushes. Then — then, oh, then — she may forget that I am the peasant's son!

Lady Windermere's Fan

Oscar Wilde

20–30

Dramatic

Lord Darlington, a cad, does his best to seduce the virtuous Lady Windermere.

Between men and women there is no friendship possible. There is passion, enmity, worship, love, but no friendship. I love you — [. . .]

Yes, I love you! You are more to me than anything in the whole world. What does your husband give you? Nothing. Whatever is in him he gives to this wretched woman, whom he has thrust into your society, into your home, to shame you before everyone. I offer you my life — [. . .]

My life — my whole life. Take it, and do with it what you will. . . . I love you — love you as I have never loved any living thing. From the moment I met you I loved you, loved you blindly, adoringly, madly! You did not know it then — you know it now! Leave this house to-night. I won't tell you that the world matters nothing, or the world's voice, or the voice of society. They matter a good deal. They matter far too much. But there are moments when one has to choose between living one's own life, fully, entirely, completely — or dragging out some false, shallow, degrading existence that the world in its hypocrisy demands. You have that moment now. Choose! Oh, my love, choose!

La Parisienne

Henry Becque

Translated by Charles Marowitz

30s

Comic

Du Mensnil impresses with his career aspirations.

I'm doing quite well at the Farm Board, you know. I've moved from pork bellies into harvesting and manure. I write regularly for their monthly bulletin. A few weeks back I caused a sensation with my article on innoculating chickens against the chicken pox. My name is on everyone's lips there. But Jean-Baptiste doesn't approve. He thinks I'm made for higher things and now that I have a wife and a child, I should find a more exalted position. I'm not a scientist or a statistician — that's not me. I'm really more of an intellectual, I suppose. Did you ever read my paper on "The Metaphysical Implications of Pork Belly Farming?" "The Psychosomatic Origins of Foot-and-Mouth Disease?" They're not for the masses, of course; they're not potboilers. Very much for a select minority. To date, both combined have sold one hundred and nineteen copies — one hundred and eighteen really — one was eaten by a parrot at the last county fair. Terrible incident actually; believe the bird choked to death shortly afterward. Nothing to do with the content, of course; the newsprint didn't agree with it, or something. — I sort of visualize a whole new field for myself where I could really come into my own.

La Parisienne

Henry Becque

Translated by Charles Marowitz

40s

Comic

Lafont justifies his infidelity by convincing himself his wife deserves such retaliation.

I must calm down. Make up my mind that it's done with and act accordingly. You can't keep a semi-respectable mistress in this town. The more respectable she is, the less chance you have of keeping her. I'll have it out with Clotilde once and for all and break with her for good. Here I am looking for her this way and that, and there she is running hither and thither. What's the point? I know damn well she's become Mercier's mistress. It's as clear as the stupid nose on my face; that nose which she so enjoys tweaking. Well, her "tweaking days" are over. Probably cares as little for Mercier as she did for me. — Some consolation! If Adolph were here, at least we could spend some time together. Play cards, or chat, or something. Whenever she makes me miserable, there's no one like Adolph to revive my spirits. When I think of his situation, I'm somewhat consoled to my own. His is far worse than mine, of course. She wrongs me at every turn. But she's wronging him as well. I can see exactly what he has to put up with. We're really both in the same boat, he and I. Here I am, desolate, cast out by her, unfriended by him, sick at heart about a ridiculous situation which gets worse and worse the longer I'm in it. What a cross we men have to bear! Either bachelors or cuckolds. — What a bloody choice!!!

La Ronde

Arthur Schnitzler

Translated by Carl R. Mueller

45+

Seriocomic

The Count wakes fully dressed on the divan. In the bed lies a prostitute. He remembers little.

(*Stirs, rubs his eyes, sits up quickly, looks around.*) How did I get — Oh! Yes. Then I did go home with that girl. (*He rises quickly and sees her in bed.*) And there she is. Imagine! A thing like that happening to a man my age! I can't remember. Did they carry me up here? No. I saw — I came into the room. Yes. I was still awake. Or — or does this room remind me of somewhere else? My God! Yes! Yes! I saw it last night. *(Looks at his watch.)* Hm. Last night. A couple of hours ago. But I knew something had to happen. I felt it. Last night when I began drinking, I felt that something — and what did happen? Nothing. Or did I — ? My God! I haven't — I haven't forgotten anything that's happened to me in ten years! Well. In any case, I was drunk. If only I could remember when it began. At least I remember when I went into that whores' cafe with Lulu and — No. No. It was after we left the Sacher. And then on the way — yes, that's right. I was riding along with Lulu. But why am I racking my brains! It doesn't matter! Just get yourself out of here! (*He rises; the lamp shakes.*) Oh! (*He looks at the sleeping girl.*) At least she's sleeping soundly — I can't remember a thing. But I'll put the money on the night table just in case. And so good-bye. (*He stands looking at her face for a long while.*)

La Ronde

Arthur Schnitzler

Translated by Carl R. Mueller

30s

Dramatic

Anatol is tortured by his wife-to-be's past and wracked with doubt about her fidelity.

Emilie! This is the eve of our wedding day! I truly believed that we'd wiped out the past. Completely. That — that when the two of us sorted through your letters, and fans and the thousand and one little nothings that reminded me of the time before I knew you — and threw them into the fireplace — and then the bracelets, and rings, and earrings that we gave away, that we threw over the bridge into the river or out the window onto the street — and then you kneeling, swearing that it was all past — that you had discovered the meaning of true love only in my arms — and naturally I believed you — because we always believe what women tell us, from the first lie that transports us to paradise — I'm through. Through with you! Oh, how cleverly you played your part. Pretending you wanted to wash away all the stains of your past, you stood here in front of the fireplace watching the papers, and ribbons, and whatnots go up in flame. And how you sobbed in my arms the time we walked along the river and tossed the precious bracelet into the gray water and watched it sink. How you wept. Purifying tears. Tears of contrition. All of it a stupid farce. And for what. For nothing. I still mistrusted you. And here's the evidence. Why don't you say something? Why don't you defend yourself?

Leonce and Lena

Georg Büchner

Translated by Henry J. Schmidt

20s

Seriocomic

Prince Leonce, a foolish young man. Privilege and sloth have turned Leonce into a fop. Here, he lazily contemplates his feelings for Rosetta.

(*Alone.*) Love is a peculiar thing. You lie half-asleep in bed for a year, then one fine morning you wake up, drink a glass of water, get dressed, and run your hand across your forehead and come to your senses — and come to your senses. — My God, how many women does one need to sing up and down the scale of love? One woman is scarcely enough for a single note. Why is the mist above the earth a prism that breaks the white-hot ray of love into a rainbow? — (*He drinks.*) Which bottle contains the wine that will make me drunk today? Can't I even get that far anymore? It's as if I were sitting under a vacuum pump. The air so sharp and thin that I'm freezing, as if I were going ice skating in cotton pants. — Gentlemen, gentlemen, do you know what Caligula and Nero were? I know. — Come, Leonce, let's have a soliloquy, I'll listen. My life yawns at me like a large white sheet of paper that I have to fill, but I can't write a single letter. My head is an empty dance hall, a few withered roses and crumpled ribbons on the floor, broken violins in the corner, the last dancers have taken off their masks and look at each other with dead-tired eyes. I turn myself inside out twenty-four times a day, like a glove. Oh, I know myself, I know what I'll be thinking and dreaming in a quarter of an hour, in a week, in a year. God, what have I done that you make me recite my lesson so often like a schoolboy? — Bravo, Leonce! Bravo! (*He applauds.*) It does me good to cheer for myself like this. Hey! Leonce! Leonce!

The Liars

Henry Arthur Jones

50s

Comic

When his friend, Ned, plans to run off with the very married Lady Jessica, Sir Christopher — a clever and philosophical man — does his best to talk them both out of their foolish passion.

Now! I've nothing to say in the abstract against running away with another man's wife! There may be planets where it is not only the highest ideal morality, but where it has the further advantage of being a practical way of carrying on society. But it has this one fatal defect in our country to-day — it won't work! You know what we English are, Ned. We're not a bit better than our neighbours, but, thank God! we do pretend we are, and we do make it hot for anybody who disturbs that holy pretence. And take my word for it, my dear Lady Jessica, my dear Ned, it won't work. You know it's not an original experiment you're making. It has been tried before. Have you ever known it to be successful? Lady Jessica, think of the brave pioneers who have gone before you in this enterprise. They've all perished, and their bones whiten the anti-matrimonial shore. Think of them! Charley Gray and Lady Rideout, [. . .] Poor old Fitz and his beauty [. . .], Billy Dover and Polly Atchison [. . .]. George Nuneham and Mrs. Sandys — George is conducting a tramcar in New York, and Mrs Sandys — Lady Jessica, you knew Mrs. Sandys, a delicate sweet little creature, I've met her at your receptions—she drank herself to death, and died in a hospital. [. . .] Not encouraging, is it? [. . .] Do believe me, my dear Ned, my dear Lady Jessica, before it is too late, do believe me, it won't work, it won't work, it won't work!

The Libation Bearers

Aeschylus

Translated by Carl R. Mueller

20s–30s

Dramatic

Orestes stands over the bodies of his mother, Klytaimnestra, and her lover, Aigisthos, with drawn sword. He has killed them both to avenge his father.

Behold the land's tyrants!
Behold the double tyranny of Argos!
The demons who raped my house,
        who plundered my rights, and murdered my father!

What majesties they once were,
        high on their thrones,
                loving partners then,
                loving partners now,
        as their fate must show,
                loving partners in suffering.
They swore an oath once to catch-up my father,
        to slaughter him, kill him in his bath,
        both together, as one, united.
And now another oath comes true,
        to die as one,
        to die together,
                lovers united even in death,
        their lofty bed now a lowly grave. [. . .]

Medeia

Euripides

Translated by Carl R. Mueller

30s

Dramatic

Jason, husband of the exiled Medeia, scolds his wife for making too much of his infidelity, thus bringing exile upon herself and their children.

This is not the first time, Medeia, but one of many, when I have had driven home to me the impossibility of dealing with a surly temper! This land, this house, could have been yours, yours forever! But no! No! You had to impose yourself, you had to have your way, make your position known! Nonsense! You and your foolish babble! So where does that put you with those who hold power? Exile is where! Oh, it means nothing to me. Be my guest, go on calling Jason the most reprehensible, the basest of men. Why should I care? But this verbal attack on the royal family is not to be endured, and you should count yourself lucky to have come off with only exile.

I did everything I could on numerous occasions to mollify their majesties' animus against you, because I wanted you to stay. But no, no, you insisted on your continuous attack of reviling the ruling house. And for that you are now exiled. Nonetheless, I am here despite your abuse and have in no way relinquished my obligations to my loved ones. I come here with one purpose in mind. Your interest and those of your children, for I don't want you to go penniless and unprovided into exile. Exile brings hardships enough on its own. However you may hate me, I could never wish you any ill will.

Medeia

Euripides

Translated by Carl R. Mueller

30s–40s

Dramatic

Jason is beyond angry. His wife, Medeia, for reasons he cannot fathom, has killed their children.

You, you detestable, you evil, most hateful of creatures to the gods, to me, to the race of men, how can you raise a sword against your own children? I'm destroyed! I have no children! Childless! And here you are, still alive, in the light of the sun, walking the earth, you who did these most abominable deeds, their mother! And I curse you! My mind is clear now, but I was insane when I brought you from your home in a barbarian land to a house in Greece, you evilest of evil monsters, a traitor to your father and home and country, the land that raised you!

[. . .] And yet I married you over all the other women of Greece, a marriage founded on hate and destruction. And got? Not a woman, but a monster, a she-lion with a nature more savage than Tyrrhenian Scylla! But ten thousand insults couldn't disturb you, so deeply perverse is your nature!

Get out of here, you artful contriver of destruction! Self-polluted with your own children's blood! Leave me to mourn my destiny. No joy will come of my new marriage; I will never again speak to my children alive, the children I fathered and raised, the children I have now lost.

Mercadet

Honoré de Balzac

Translated by Robert Cornthwaite

30+

Comic

Mercadet is a financier who swindles investors.

You don't know these times! Nowadays, madame, there are no traditional values. Who determines what the crown jewels of England are worth? The King? The public who worship the crown and its age-old history? No, an insurance company! People put their faith in funds. A girl gets her dowry from an annuity. A wife relies on her investments, not on her husband. Servants are loyal only if you have their money — and hang on to it. [. . .]

(*Taking out a five-franc piece.*) Here is honor for you — modern honor. Do you know why plays with rascals for heroes are so successful? Because they flatter the audience, who say, "Well! I'm not as bad as that crook!" [. . .]

I'm simply the scapegoat. I take the blame for Godeau, who absconded with our company funds. And after all, what's so disgraceful about owing money? Aren't we all in debt — the child to the father who gave him life? The earth to the sun? Life, madame, is a perpetual borrowing — and never paying back. I'm better off than my creditors, am I not? I have their money; they only yearn for mine. They're obsessed with me! Nobody gives a thought to the man who owes nothing, while my creditors think about me day and night!

The Merchant of Venice

William Shakespeare

40+

Dramatic

Shylock makes the case for equal justice for Jews and Christians.

He hath disgraced me, and hindered me half a million; laughed at my losses, mocked at my gains, scorned my nation, thwarted my bargains, cooled my friends, heated mine enemies; and what's his reason? I am a Jew.

Hath not a Jew eyes? Hath not a Jew hands, organs, dimensions, senses, affections, passions? Fed with the same food, hurt with the same weapons, subject to the same diseases, healed by the same means, warmed and cooled by the same winter and summer, as a Christian is?

If you prick us, do we not bleed? If you tickle us, do we not laugh? If you poison us, do we not die? And if you wrong us, shall we not revenge? If we are like you in the rest, we will resemble you in that.

If a Jew wrong a Christian, what is his humility . . . ? Revenge.

If a Christian wrong a Jew, what should his sufferance be by Christian example? Why, revenge.

The villany you teach me, I will execute, and it shall go hard . . . but I will better the instruction.

Michaelmas Term

Thomas Middleton

20–30

Seriocomic

England. Hellgill, a panderer, does his best to convince a country wench to provide amorous services for his master.

Wouldst thou, a pretty, beautiful, juicy squall, live in a poor thrum'd house i'th' country in such servile habiliments, and may well pass for a gentlewoman i'th' city? Does not five hundred do so, think'st thou, and with worse faces? Oh, now in these latter days, the devil reigning, 'tis an age for cloven creatures. But why sad now? Yet indeed 'tis the fashion of any courtesan to be seasick i'th' first voyage, but at next she proclaims open wars, like a beaten soldier. Why, Northamptonshire lass, dost dream of virginity now? Remember a loose-bodied gown, wench, and let it go; wires and tires, bents and bums, felts and falls, thou shalt deceive the world, that gentlewomen indeed shall not be known from others. I have a master to whom I must prefer thee after the aforesaid decking, Lethe by name, a man of one most admired property: he can both love thee, and for thy better advancement be thy pander himself, an exc'llent spark of humility.

A Midsummer Night's Dream

William Shakespeare

20+

Comic

Puck taunts us with the possibility that the story we've just watched was "but a dream."

If we shadows have offended,
Think but this, and all is mended,
That you have but slumber'd here
While these visions did appear.
And this weak and idle theme,
No more yielding but a dream,
Gentles, do not reprehend:
if you pardon, we will mend:
And, as I am an honest Puck,
If we have unearned luck
Now to 'scape the serpent's tongue,
We will make amends ere long;
Else the Puck a liar call;
So, good night unto you all.
Give me your hands, if we be friends,
And Robin shall restore amends.

A Midsummer Night's Dream

William Shakespeare

35+

Comic

Duke Theseus makes the comparison between those in love and the mentally disturbed.

Lovers and madmen have such seething brains,
Such shaping fantasies, that apprehend
More than cool reason ever comprehends.
The lunatic, the lover, and the poet
Are of imagination all compact.
One sees more devils than vast hell can hold;
That is the madman. The lover, all as frantic,
Sees Helen's beauty in a brow of Egypt.
The poet's eye, in a fine frenzy rolling,
Doth glance from heaven to earth, from earth to heaven.
And as imagination bodies forth
The forms of things unknown, the poet's pen
Turns them to shapes, and gives to airy nothing
A local habitation, and a name.
Such tricks hath strong imagination,
That if it would but apprehend some joy,
It comprehends some bringer of that joy.
Or in the night, imagining some fear,
How easy is a bush supposed a bear.

The Molluse

Hubert Henry Davies

20–30

Seriocomic

Tom, a young man possessed of keen insight into life, is a member of an eccentric family he claims resembles molluscs.

She's a mollusc. [. . .]
Mollusca, subdivision of the animal kingdom. [. . .]
People who are like a mollusc of the sea, which clings to a rock and lets the tide flow over its head. People instead of moving, in whom the instinct for what I call molluscry is as dominating as an inborn vice. And it is so catching. Why, one mollusc will infect a whole household. We all had it at home. Mother was quite a famous mollusc in her time. She was bedridden for fifteen years, and then, don't you remember, got up to Dulcie's wedding, to the amazement of everybody, and tripped down the aisle as lively as a kitten, and then went to bed again till she heard of something else she wanted to go to — a garden party or something. Father, he was a mollusc, too; he called it being a conservative; he might just as well have stayed in bed, too. Ada, Charlie, Emmeline, all of them were more or less mollusky, but Dulcibella was the queen. You won't often see such a fine healthy specimen of a mollusc as Dulcie. I'm a born mollusc.

Money

Edward Bulwer-Lytton

30–40

Seriocomic

Graves, a recent widower and a man of caustic sensibilities, expresses his dislike of newspapers.

Ay — read the newspapers! — They'll tell you what this world is made of. Daily calendars of roguery and woe! Here, advertisements from quacks, money-lenders, cheap warehouses, and spotted boys with two heads! So much for dupes and impostors! Turn to the other column — police reports, bankruptcies, swindling, forgery, and a biographical sketch of the snub-nosed man who murdered his own three little cherubs at Pentonville. Do you fancy these but exceptions to the general virtue and health of the nation? — Turn to the leading article! and your hair will stand on end at the horrible wickedness or melancholy idiotism of that half of the population who think differently from yourself. In my day I have seen already eighteen crises, six annihilations of agriculture and commerce, four overthrows of the Church, and three last, final, awful, and irremediable destructions of the entire Constitution! And that's a newspaper — a newspaper — a newspaper!

Much Ado about Nothing

William Shakespeare

20s

Seriocomic

Messina. Benedick, a young lord of Padua. When Benedick's friend Claudio falls in love, Benedick contemplates the strange changes that love can make in the heart of a man.

I do much wonder that one man, seeing how much another man is a fool when he dedicates his behaviours to love, will, after he hath laughed at such shallow follies in others, become the argument of his own scorn by falling in love: and such a man is Claudio. I have known when there was no music with him but the drum and the fife; and now had he rather hear the tabor and the pipe: I have known when he would have walked ten mile a-foot to see a good armour; and now will he lie ten nights awake, carving the fashion of a new doublet. He was wont to speak plain and to the purpose, like an honest man and a soldier; and now is he turned orthography; his words are a very fantastical banquet, just so many strange dishes. May I be so converted and see with these eyes? I cannot tell; I think not: I will not be sworn but love may transform me to an oyster; but I'll take my oath on it, till he have made an oyster of me, he shall never make me such a fool. One woman is fair, yet I am well; another is wise, yet I am well; another virtuous, yet I am well; but till all graces be in one woman, one woman shall not come in my grace. Rich she shall be, that's certain; wise, or I'll none; virtuous, or I'll never cheapen her; fair, or I'll never look on her; mild, or come not near me; noble, or not I for an angel; of good discourse, an excellent musician, and her hair shall be of what colour it please God.

The Octoroon

Dion Boucicault

30s

Dramatic

To possess the beautiful Zoe, McClusky — an evil slave owner — murders the mail carrier who was bringing evidence of her status as a freed slave. When his crime is discovered, he escapes into the bayou where he is pursued by justice and nightmares.

Burn, burn! blaze away! How the flames crack. I'm not guilty; would ye murder me? Cut, cut the rope — I choke — choke! Ah! (*Wakes.*) Hello! where am I? Why, I was dreaming — curse it! I can never sleep now without dreaming. Hush! I thought I heard the sound of a paddle in the water. All night, as I fled through the canebrake, I heard footsteps behind me. I lost them in the cedar swamp — again they haunted my path down the bayou, moving as I moved, resting when I rested — hush! there again! — no; it was only the wind over the canes. The sun is rising. I must launch my dug-out, and put for the bay, and in a few hours I shall be safe from pursuit on board of one of the coasting schooners that run from Galveston to Matagorda. In a little time this darned business will blow over, and I can show again. Hark! there's that noise again! If it was the ghost of that murdered boy haunting me! Well — I didn't mean to kill him, did I? Well, then, what has my all-cowardly heart got to skeer me so for?

Oedipus Tyrannos

Sophokles

Translated by Carl R. Mueller and Anna Krajewska-Wieczorek

20s–30s

Dramatic

Oedipus, King of Thebes, has fulfilled a prophecy by unknowingly murdering his father and marrying his mother. After blinding himself, he calls his daughters to him and wishes them a better life.

I weep for you now, who cannot see you,
Thinking of the bitter life of sorrow
That men will force on you. What assemblies
Of citizens will you not join: what Theban festivals
Will you not attend, except to turn back,
To return home in tears, instead of enjoying
The celebration? And when it is time to marry,
What man will risk the burden of infamy
That will haunt you because you are my children?
What evil won't you know?
Your father killed his father,
Seeded the womb that bore him,
The same womb that bore you.
These are the insults you will have to bear.
Who will marry you then? No one, my children.
You will wither away, unmarried, barren fields —
Without children. [. . .]

Children! If only you could understand,
If only you were old enough to know,
I would have so much to tell you. As it is,
This is the prayer that I would have you pray:
To find a place to live and have a life
Better than your poor father ever knew.

Oedipus Tyrannos

Sophokles

Translated by Carl R. Mueller and Anna Krajewska-Wieczorek

30s

Dramatic

When Oedipus, King of Thebes, fulfills a prophecy by unknowingly murdering his father and marrying his mother, he exacts vengeance upon himself. Here, a Messenger describes the scene.

Oedipus burst in a rage
On the room with a terrible cry,
There we saw her — hanging,
Swaying in a mass of twisted cords;
And seeing this, a roar rose from his breast
That broke our hearts; and then he slipped the noose
From around her neck and in his arms lowered
Her body to the floor; and when, poor woman,
She lay on the ground, so terrible a scene was played,
I wish I didn't remember!

He tore the two gold pins that fastened her dress,
And seeing her there, raised high the pins,
One in each hand, and plunged them deep into his eyes,
Crying that they would never again see
The misery of his fate, the horrors of his deeds,
Eyes that from here onward, in the dark,
Must look on those that they should never have seen,
And never again see those they long to see.
And as his chanting soared, his hands brought down

Grief after grief on his eyes, strike upon strike,
Opening wide his lids to welcome more,
Till his whole face streamed not with drops,
But with dark currents of gore that pulsed from his eyes.

Prosperity once reigned in this house.
Happiness, success, were truly theirs.
And yet today, on this day,
Mourning, ruin, death, disgrace,
All, every evil, has come
To dwell in these walls.

On the Harmful Effects of Tobacco

Anton Chekhov

Translated by Carol Rocamora

35+

Comic

Ivan Ivanovich Nyukhin, husband of the proprietress of a music conservatory and boarding school for young ladies. The scene takes place on the dais of an auditorium in a provincial club. Enter Nyukhin, wearing long side-whiskers, with no moustache, and an old, threadbare tailcoat. He strides in majestically, bows, and adjusts his waistcoat.

Ladies, and, in a manner of speaking, gentlemen. (*Combs his whiskers.*) It has been suggested to my wife that I deliver a public lecture here today for charitable purposes. Well, why not? If I'm supposed to lecture, I'll lecture. It's all the same to me, really. I mean, I'm not a professor, well of course I'm not, in fact, I have no academic degree of any kind, but, nevertheless, and be that as it may, I have worked these past thirty years, worked without cease, I might very well add, to the detriment of my own health and so on and so forth, worked on issues of purest science, reflecting upon them, even writing scholarly articles on them from time to time, if you can imagine, well not exactly scholarly, but, if you'll pardon the expression, sort of scholarly, so to speak. Incidentally, I wrote a very extensive article recently, entitled: "Certain insects and their adverse effects." My daughters liked it very much, particularly the part about the bedbugs, but then I reread it and tore it to pieces. Because it's all the same in the end, really, you know, whether you write articles or not, you just can't get by without insect powder. We've even got bed-bugs in the piano . . . I have chosen, as it were, for the topic of today's lecture: the harmful effects of tobacco on humans. Now I myself am a smoker, but my wife has instructed me to talk about the harmfulness of tobacco today, and so, as they say, that's that. If it's tobacco, then it's tobacco — really, I couldn't care less, but I do ask you, distinguished ladies and gentlemen, to try to take my lecture today as seriously as you possibly can, or else I shall suffer the consequences.

On the Harmful Effects of Tobacco

Anton Chekhov

Translated by Carol Rocamora

35+

Comic

Ivan Ivanovich Nyukhin, husband of the proprietress of a music conservatory and boarding school for young ladies. The scene takes place on the dais of an auditorium in a provincial club. Nyukhin has been forced to deliver this lecture.

I have chosen, as it were, for the topic of today's lecture: the harmful effects of tobacco on humans. Now I myself am a smoker, but my wife has instructed me to talk about the harmfulness of tobacco today, and so, as they say, that's that. If it's tobacco, then it's tobacco — really, I couldn't care less, but I do ask you, distinguished ladies and gentlemen, to try to take my lecture today as seriously as you possibly can, or else I shall suffer the consequences. And whosoever is put off by pure scientific discourse, then by all means, he or she is absolutely free to leave. (*Adjusts his waistcoat.*) I would, however, specifically like to call to attention any doctors who might be present, who might glean from my lecture some particularly useful information, inasmuch as tobacco, apart from its harmful effects, also has practical medical application. For example, if we were to place a fly into a snuffbox, then it would most likely die from a nervous disorder. Tobacco is considered, for the most part, to be a plant . . . When I give a lecture, I find that my right eye tends to twitch, so please, pay no attention to it, it's because I'm nervous. I'm a very nervous person, generally speaking, and my eye started twitching on the thirteenth of September, 1889, the very same day upon which my wife gave birth, so to speak, to our fourth daughter, Varvara. All my daughters were born on the thirteenth day of the month. However (*Looks at his watch.*) in view of the shortage of time, let us not stray from the subject of our lecture.

On the Harmful Effects of Tobacco

Anton Chekhov
Translated by Carol Rocamora

35+
Comic

Ivan Ivanovich Nyukhin, husband of the proprietress of a music conservatory and boarding school for young ladies, is forced to deliver this lecture — but he is frequently distracted.

Tobacco is considered, for the most part, to be a plant . . . When I give a lecture, I find that my right eye tends to twitch, so please, pay no attention to it, it's because I'm nervous. I'm a very nervous person, generally speaking, and my eye started twitching on the thirteenth of September, 1889, the very same day upon which my wife gave birth, so to speak, to our fourth daughter, Varvara. All my daughters were born on the thirteenth day of the month. However (*Looks at his watch.*) in view of the shortage of time, let us not stray from the subject of our lecture. At this time I should call to your attention that my wife runs both a music conservatory and a private boarding school, well, not exactly a boarding school, but something along those lines. [. . .] I manage the housekeeping department in the boarding school. I buy the supplies, supervise the servants, keep the accounts, stitch the copy books, get rid of the bedbugs, walk my wife's dog, catch the mice . . . Last evening, it was my responsibility to provide the cook with flour and oil, because we were having blinis. Well, today, to make a long story short, after the blinis were already made, my wife came into the kitchen to inform us that three of the pupils would not be eating blinis, because they had swollen glands. And, so it seems, we found ourselves with an overabundance of blinis. What were we supposed to do with them? At first, my wife ordered me to store them in the cellar, but she thought for a moment, and then she said: "Oh, go eat them yourself, dummy." That's what she calls me when she's in a bad mood: dummy. Or viper. Or Satan. Where did she get "Satan" from? She's always in a bad mood.

On the Harmful Effects of Tobacco

Anton Chekhov

Translated by Carol Rocamora

35+

Comic

Ivan Ivanovich Nyukhin, husband of the proprietress of a music conservatory and boarding school for young ladies, is forced to deliver this lecture — but he is frequently distracted and he unloads his misery upon his audience.

Our music conservatory is located on Five Dogs Lane, Number 13. That's why I've been so unlucky in life, in all likelihood, because we live at House Number 13. And my daughters were all born on the thirteenth day of the month, and our house has thirteen windows . . . Oh, what's the use of talking about it! [. . .] That's right, house number thirteen! Nothing has worked out for me in life, I've gotten older, and duller . . . Here I am, delivering a lecture to you, with a great big smile on my face, but deep down inside I want to scream at the top of my lungs, I want to fly away to the ends of the earth. I want to weep . . . and I've no one to tell my troubles to . . . What about my daughters, you say . . . Well, what about them? When I try to talk to them, they only laugh in my face . . . My wife has seven daughters . . . No, sorry, six . . . (*Quickly.*) Seven! [. . .] I've been married to my wife for thirty-three years, and I can safely say that these have been the best years of my life, well, maybe not exactly the best, but something along those lines. They have flown by, in a word, like one happy moment, so to speak, and curse them all, curse them. (*Glances around.*) Anyway, she still hasn't arrived, she's not here yet, so I can say whatever I like . . .

Oresteia

Aeschylus

Translated by Carl R. Mueller

40s

Dramatic

At Aulis, Agamemnon is waiting in vain for the winds to cease so that the fleet may set sail for Troy. He is confronted with the prophet's demand that he kill his own daughter.

I have a duty,
and that duty is obedience,
and that obedience is my doom,
obedience to the gods!
But obedience to myself and my love,
what of that?
If I massacre my daughter,
the ships sail and we reach Troy.
But if I massacre my daughter, the pride of my house,
my joy,
my love,
what am I to myself but a monster,
and a monster to all the world?
It is a heavy price either way.
How am I to desert my ships,
my fleet,
desert my allies,
when they have every right to demand the sacrifice?
The blood of a virgin for the winds to cease,
the ships to sail,
to reach Troy.

And it is right in the eyes of the gods.
Their anger is just,
the rage of my men,
and am I not bound?
But how am I to kill my child,
stain my hands,
a father's hands, make them stream with a virgin's blood,
a daughter's blood,
make an altar run with her blood,
for the gods to see?
That is not right in the eyes of the gods.
But so be it.

Orestes

Euripides

Translated by Carl R. Mueller

20–30

Dramatic

Following the advice of the god Apollo, Orestes has killed his mother, Klytaimnestra, and her lover to avenge the death of his father at her hands. Wracked with the blood-guilt of matricide, he questions his fundamental beliefs. He speaks to his grandfather, Tyndaraeos.

I tremble at your age, dear old man. And yet I must — I must speak. What was I to do? [. . .]

I hated my mother, yes, and my hatred was justified. She betrayed him, betrayed her husband, away from home, at arms, commander of the combined forces of Greece, and she polluted his bed with an unholy alliance. And knowing she was guilty, did she punish herself? No. Rather to avoid punishment by her husband, she punished him, killed him, killed my father! By all the gods — or should I shrink from mentioning gods, for it's they who sit in judgment over murder — but what if I had said nothing, in silence condoned my mother's action, what would *he* have done to me, *he*, my father's ghost, my murdered father's ghost? Hounded me, driven me insane with the Furies bound with a father's hatred! Or is it only my mother is avenged by gods and he with no gods at all, and his hurt the greater?

And what's this? Forgotten Apollo? Delphi's god that sits at earth's navel? Apollo we obey blindly? Apollo whose command was to kill her, to kill my mother? Should he not be accused, the immoral god? Should he not be put to death for his crime? Kill him! Kill the guilty one! The sin's not mine, it's his! What was I to do? Is the god not worth his word to clear me of pollution? Where do I turn, to whom, when the god who ordered me to murder will not save me? *You*, sir, it was *you* who destroyed me, *you*, when you fathered an evil daughter. Thanks to her, to her brazen audacity, I've lost my father and killed my mother for it! No, no one must say what I did was wrong, but only that I who did it ended in misery.

Persians

Aeschylus

Translated by Carl R. Mueller

45+

Dramatic

When the Ghost of Dareios rises from his grave, he speaks in no uncertain terms of the stupidity of his son's flagrant defiance of the gods' law that keeps man in check and of the consequences if man fails to obey.

How swiftly god's oracles work!
How swiftly Zeus hurls it
    down upon my son! I had
hoped for more time,
        the distant future,
but when a man is a fool and loses control,
    the gods speed him on his way.
            A well of disaster
    overflows for all I love.
And this was my son's doing,
    this his achievement, who in his
impetuous youth sought,
    like a slave, blindly, to
chain the sacred flowing Hellespont,
    god's holy spring, the Bosporos.
He made land of the sea,
    against all nature,
laying a great road for his great army.
How foolish to think he could master the
        gods, including Poseidon.

What was it but some disease that gripped his
mind?
Now all I fought to win,
the gold, the power,
are left to be plundered by anyone who wills.

The Prince of Homburg

Heinrich von Kleist

Translated by Carl R. Mueller

20–30

Dramatic

The Prince, speaking to the Electress, falls apart when faced with his death sentence.

On my way here I passed the grave that will hold me tomorrow. I saw it gaping at me in the torchlight. Tomorrow these eyes will be dark. This body shot through. And all the windows on the square are rented for the spectacle! I who have everything to live for today, tomorrow will lie stinking between two boards, a stone at my head as proof that I once existed. [. . .] But the world is such a beautiful place! I don't want to die! That time will come soon enough! If I've sinned, let him punish me. Just not with bullets. He can strip me of my offices, discharge me from the army! Dear God, since I saw my grave all I want is to live! Even in dishonor! I don't care any more! [. . .]

You and my mother were friends. When she died, she gave me to you, asked you to care for me as a mother. You knelt at her bedside, you kissed her hand, and you promised. I remind you now of that promise. Go to him now and beg his mercy. Beg him to set me free. And then come back and tell me that I'm free.

The Prince of Parthia

Thomas Godfrey

20s

Dramatic

1767. Sullen Vardanes, the Prince of Parthia, reveals his hatred of his brother, Arsaces, who is the king's favorite.

I hate *Arsaces*,
Tho' he's my Mother's son, and churchmen say
There's something sacred in the name of Brother.
My soul endures him not, and he's the bane
Of all my hopes of greatness. Like the sun
He rules the day, and like the night's pale Queen,
My fainter beams are lost when he appears.
And this because he came into the world,
A moon or two before me: What's the diff'rence,
That he alone should shine in Empire's seat?
I am not apt to trumpet forth my praise.
Or highly name myself, but this I'll speak,
To him in ought, I'm not the least inferior.
Ambition, glorious fever! mark of Kings,
Gave me immortal thirst and rule of Empire.
Why lag'd my tardy soul, why droop'd the wing,
Nor forward springing, shot before his speed
To seize the prize? — 'Twas Empire —
Oh! 'twas Empire —

Prometheus Bound

Aeschylus

Translated by Carl R. Mueller

25+

Dramatic

Prometheus, cast away by Zeus, rejects any offers to "make nice" with him and enumerates to the chorus all his contributions to mankind.

You think me stubborn, do you?
Stiff-necked, proud, arrogant?
Because I am silent,
        because I say nothing?
                        No.
Not true.
        My heart is eaten away with
        painful brooding at the outrage
                I'm made to suffer,
        the brutality, the humiliation.
[. . .]
Listen at least to this.
Listen to how men's minds were empty,
        how they were helpless as babies,
        and how I brought them thought,
                the power to reason,
        I brought them intelligence.
[. . .]
They had eyes,
        but did not see,
        ears, but did not hear.

They dragged their way through their
long burden of days like figures in
dreams, confused,
directionless.

[. . .]

I showed them how the stars moved through the sky,
their risings and their settings; no easy
text to decipher.
I gave them numbers then,
my own invention,
of all skills the most useful,
mathematics.
And letters,
the servant of memory,
eternal storehouse of knowledge,
mother of arts.

[. . .]

These were the gifts I gave to man — I who have no
cleverness to escape this agony of my own.

The Provoked Wife

Sir John Vanbrugh

20s

Seriocomic

1697, England. Sir John, a man chafing in his marriage, can no longer tolerate his wife.

What cloying meat is love, when matrimony's the sauce to it. Two years' marriage has debauched my five senses. Everything I see, everything I hear, everything I feel, everything I smell, and everything I taste, methinks has wife in't. No boy was ever so weary of his tutor, no girl of her bib, no nun of doing penance, nor old maid of being chaste, as I am of being married. Sure there's a secret curse entailed upon the very name of wife. My lady is a young lady, a fine lady, a witty lady, a virtuous lady, and yet I hate her. There is but one thing on earth I loathe beyond her: that's fighting. Would my courage come up but to a fourth part of my ill nature, I'd stand buff to her relations, and thrust her out of doors. But marriage has sunk me down to such an ebb of resolution, I dare not draw my sword, though even to get rid of my wife. But here she comes.

Quack

Charles Marowitz

A musical version of *The Physician in Spite of Himself* by Molière

40s

Comic

Orville, posing as a doctor, flaunts his lack of knowledge.

Aristotle has written a long discourse on precisely that subject. You haven't read it by any chance? A great man, Aristotle. A great man. He came up to about here I'd say. (*Raises his hand to indicate height.*) On some days, he was even taller. One of those men who the more knowledge he acquired, the greater he became. His view was — this was many years ago mind you — he's since been superceded by much greater men — (*Raises his hand to indicate their height.*) — that the obstruction was caused by certain humors, or as you might say tumors, which were of an unwholesome nature that came about because of vapors, or as you might say capers, which affected the diseased areas by means of taking these areas and, as it were, filling them full of disease. — Let's see if I can make this simpler — Uh, do you know Latin? It's a matter of the Cabricias archi thurman, or catalmus, singulariter haec Musa — or as you might say, bonus, bona, bonum — epithalium — valium — impalium — gollywogaylium. [. . .] . . . you're following all this, aren't you?

Quack

Charles Marowitz

A musical version of *The Physician in Spite of Himself* by Molière

40s

Comic

Orville, posing as a doctor, schools young Leopold, who has joined him in a deception.

Perfect. You look just like an Interne. Just stick close and keep giving me those doe-eyed looks, and anything I say, just agree with it. [. . .] Now let's say they ask you for a medical opinion, what do you say? You say: "It may be quite serious. It might need surgery. The chances of success are fifty/fifty. It might take a year to heal up. No one can give any guarantees." Or contrariwise: "It may be nothing at all. A little medication and it will all clear up. Just have a lot of rest and eat regularly." Of course the ideal diagnosis tries to combine a little of each. "It's quite serious. It may be nothing at all. It might need major surgery; on the other hand it might clear up by itself. If it doesn't heal in a month, it may take a year." [It means] nothing, of course. But you've left all your options open. If the patient dies, you predicted it. If he gets well, you said as much. If he gets well and then he dies, you got them coming and going. Either way, you get paid.

Richard III

William Shakespeare

30s

Dramatic

Richard gloats about his use of power, lies, and crime to obtain the woman he desires, Queen Anne.

Was ever woman in this humour woo'd?
Was ever woman in this humour won?
I'll have her; but I will not keep her long.
What! I, that kill'd her husband and his father,
To take her in her heart's extremest hate,
With curses in her mouth, tears in her eyes,
The bleeding witness of her hatred by;
Having God, her conscience, and these bars
against me,
And I nothing to back my suit at all,
But the plain devil and dissembling looks,
And yet to win her, all the world to nothing!
Ha! [. . .]
My dukedom to a beggarly denier,
I do mistake my person all this while:
Upon my life, she finds, although I cannot,
Myself to be a marvellous proper man.
I'll be at charges for a looking-glass,
And entertain some score or two of tailors,
To study fashions to adorn my body:
Since I am crept in favour with myself,
Will maintain it with some little cost.
But first I'll turn yon fellow in his grave;
And then return lamenting to my love.
Shine out, fair sun, till I have bought a glass,
That I may see my shadow as I pass.

Richelieu

Edward Bulwer-Lytton

20s

Seriocomic

This dashing young Chevalier de Mauprat has fallen in love with Julie, the ward of the powerful Cardinal Richelieu. His passion gives way to poetry.

Why, man,
the thoughts of lovers stir with poetry
as leaves with summer-wind. — The heart that loves
Dwells in an Eden, hearing angel-lutes,
As Eve in the First
garden. Hast thou seen
My Julie, and not felt it henceforth dull
To live in the common world — and talk in words
That clothe the feelings of the frigid herd?
Upon the perfumed pillow of her lips —
As on his native bed of roses flushed
With Paphian skies — Love smiling sleeps: — Her voice
The blest interpreter of thoughts as pure
As virgin wells where Dian takes delight,
Or fairies dip their changelings! — In the maze
Of her harmonious beauties — Modesty
(Like some severer grace that lead the choir
Of her sweet sisters) every airy motion
Attunes to such chaste charm, that Passion holds
His burning breath, and will not with a sigh
Dissolve the spell that binds him! — Oh, those eyes
That woo the earth — shadowing more soul than lurks

Under the lids of Psyche! — Go! — thy lip
Curls at the purfled phrases of a lover —
Love thou, and if thy love be deep as mine,
Thou wilt not laugh at poets.

The Rivals

Richard Brinsley Sheridan

20s

Seriocomic

1775, Bath, England. Faulkner and Julia are bound to marry by contract. When Faulkner questions her love for him, she leaves in tears. Here, the unhappy young man calls after her.

In tears! Stay, Julia: stay but for a moment. — The door is fastened! Julia! — my soul — but for one moment. I hear her sobbing! 'Sdeath! what a brute am I to use her thus! Yet stay! — Aye — she is coming now. How little resolution there is in woman! How a few soft words can turn them! — No, faith! — she is not coming either! Why, Julia — my love — say but that you forgive me — come but to tell me that. Now, this is being too resentful. — Stay! she is coming too — I thought she would — no steadiness in anything! her going away must have been a mere trick then. She sha'nt see that I was hurt by it. I'll affect indifference. (Hums a tune: then listens.) — No — Z — ds! she's not coming! — nor don't intend it, I suppose. This is not steadiness, but obstinacy! Yet I deserve it. What, after so long an absence to quarrel with her tenderness! — 'twas barbarous and unmanly! I should be ashamed to see her now. I'll wait till her just resentment is abated — and when I distress her so again, may I lose her forever, and be linked instead to some antique virago, whose gnawing passions, and long-hoarded spleen shall make me curse my folly half the day, and all the night!

Romance

Edward Sheldon

51

Seriocomic

When Van Tuyl, a man facing middle age, discovers that the beautiful young Rita is attracted to him, he does his best to discourage her.

Rita, suppose we finish our — our friendship — end it here tonight. [. . .]

Give me your hand. There! Now we can talk! — I'm fond of you, dear — I always shall be that — but already I'm beginning to disappoint you. And I'm afraid I'll do it more and more as time goes on. (*Slight pause.*) Look at my hair! There wasn't any grey in it last year — at Millefleurs! But now — and next year there'll be more! And I've begun to be a little deaf and fall asleep in chairs and dream about tomorrow's dinner. My rheumatism, too, came back last week — (*She winces and draws away her hand.*) Don't blame me, dear — I can't help getting old. [. . .]

(*Quickly.*) God knows I'm not complaining! I've lived my life — and it's been very sweet. I've done some work, and done it pretty well, and then I've found time to enjoy a great many of the beautiful things that fill this beautiful world. (*Politely.*) Among them, my dear, I count your voice — and you! (*Resuming.*) And yet the fact remains I've lived my life, I'm in the twilight years — oh! they're golden yet, but that won't last, and they'll grow deep and dim until the last tinge of the sunset's gone and the stars are out and night comes — and it's time to sleep. (*With a change of tone.*) But you — Good Lord, your life has just begun! Why, the dew's still on the grass — it's sparkling brighter than your brightest diamonds! (*He touches the ornaments.*) The birds are singing madrigals, the meadow's burst into a sea of flowers — you wear the morning like a wreath upon your hair — don't lose all that, my dear — don't waste your springtime on a stupid fellow fifty-one years old!

Romeo and Juliet

William Shakespeare

Teens
Dramatic

Romeo spies Juliet on her balcony.

(*Juliet appears above at a window.*)
But, soft! what light through yonder window breaks?
It is the east, and Juliet is the sun.
Arise, fair sun, and kill the envious moon,
Who is already sick and pale with grief,
That thou her maid art far more fair than she:
Be not her maid, since she is envious;
Her vestal livery is but sick and green
And none but fools do wear it; cast it off.
It is my lady, O, it is my love!
O, that she knew she were!
She speaks yet she says nothing: what of that?
Her eye discourses; I will answer it.
I am too bold, 'tis not to me she speaks:
Two of the fairest stars in all the heaven,
Having some business, do entreat her eyes
To twinkle in their spheres till they return. [. . .]
See, how she leans her cheek upon her hand!
O, that I were a glove upon that hand,
That I might touch that cheek!

Salomé

Oscar Wilde

50s

Dramatic

Herod, the Tetrarch of Judaea, preparing to have his wife's daughter, Salomé, dance for him, digresses.

Now I am happy. I am passing happy. Have I not the right to be happy? Your daughter is going to dance for me. Wilt thou not dance for me, Salomé? Thou hast promised to dance for me. [. . .]

You hear what your daughter says. she is going to dance for me. Thou doest well to dance for me, Salomé. And when thou hast danced for me, forget not to ask of me whatsoever thou hast a mind to ask. Whatsoever thou shalt desire I will give it thee, even to the half of my kingdom. I have sworn it, have I not? [. . .]

And I have never broken my word. I am not of those who break their oaths. I know not how to lie. I am the slave of my word, and my word is the word of a king. The King of Cappadocia had ever a lying tongue, but he is no true king. He is a coward. Also he owes me money that he will not repay. He has even insulted my ambassadors. He has spoken words that were wounding. But Caesar will crucify him when he comes to Rome. I know that Caesar will crucify him. And if he crucify him not, yet will he die, being eaten of worms. The prophet has prophesied it. Well! wherefore dost thou tarry, Salomé?

The School for Scandal

Richard Brinsley Sheridan

40s

Seriocomic

1777, London. Sir Peter married a country woman much younger than he in hopes of sharing his life with someone as yet untainted by material desires. When his wife quickly adapts to city ways, he finds himself at his wits' end.

When an old bachelor takes a young wife, what is he to expect? — 'Tis now six months since Lady Teazle made me the happiest of men — and I have been the miserablest dog ever since that ever committed wedlock! We tift a little going to church, and came to a quarrel before the bells were done ringing. I was more than once nearly choked with gall during the honeymoon, and had lost all comfort in life before my friends had done wishing me joy! Yet I chose with caution — a girl bred wholly in the country, who never knew luxury beyond one silk gown, nor dissipation above the annual gala of a race ball. Yet now she plays her part in all the extravagent fopperies of the fashion and the town, with as ready a grace as if she had never seen a bush nor a grassplat out of Grosvenor Square! I am sneered at by my old acquaintance — paragraphed in the newspapers. She dissipates my fortune, and contradicts all my humors; yet the worst of it is, I doubt I love her, or I should never bear all this. However, I'll never be weak enough to own it.

The Seagull

Anton Chekhov

Translated by Carol Rocamora

25

Dramatic

Konstantin Gavrilovich Treplev, a young playwright, speaks of his actress mother, Madame Arkadina, and the state of the contemporary theater.

(*Plucking petals off a flower.*) She loves me, she loves me not; she loves me, she loves me not; she loves me, she loves me not. (*Laughs.*)You see, my mother doesn't love me. And why should she? She wants romance and adventure, a whole new life for herself, a gay, romantic life, and here I am, twenty-five years old, a constant reminder that she's not so young any more. When I'm not around, she's only thirty-two, and when I am, presto! — she's forty-three, and she hates me for it. She also knows I don't believe in the "theater," such as it is. She adores the theater — she thinks she's serving mankind and her sacred art, but if you ask me, our theater of today is dull and narrow-minded. Every evening, when the curtain goes up, and there under the bright lights, in a room with three walls, those celebrated artists, those high priests of our sacred art, when they play it all out before us, how we mortals eat, and drink, and love, and go around wearing our clothes and leading our lives; when out of this vulgar scenario we are served up some kind of message or moral, however meagre, ready for our daily domestic consumption; when after its one-thousandth incarnation all these plays seem to me to be the same, time after time after time the same, then I flee — I flee like Maupassant fled the Eiffel Tower, because it outraged him how enormously trite it was.

Seven against Thebes

Aeschylus

Translated by Carl R. Mueller

25+

Dramatic

Eteoklês, King of Thebes, son of Oedipus, chastises the Theban women.

Vile, insupportable creatures!
Is this how you help the
          city, your city, a city that needs
                              help? [. . .]
By throwing yourselves at the
                    feet of the city-gods' statues?
By groveling before them?
          Howling, shrieking? [. . .]
Save me from the female sex,
                    bad times or good!
Give them the upper hand and
          they're insufferable; frightened, they're a
                    danger to the home and even more
to the city!

What have you done here with your
          mad storming about but
                    drained the people's hearts of
courage and given cowardice
                              a foothold?

While the enemy successfully attacks us
outside the walls, you destroy us from
within!
It's the price we pay for living with women! [. . .]

This is men's work and
men's work it will remain!

Go inside, now,
inside with you, and stay there,
inside your houses, and make no
trouble!

Spring's Awakening

Frank Wedekind

Translated by Carl R. Mueller

Teens

Seriocomic

Moritz's best friend Melchior has shown him an essay he has written about sexual intercourse. It profoundly affects Moritz.

That's how I've felt since I read your essay. It slipped out of my French grammar just after vacation started. God, I must've read most of it with my eyes closed! The way you explained it was like I knew it all before I was born, and then forgot it when I came into the world. What hit me hardest was the part about girls. I'll never forget that. Believe me, Melchior, it's better to suffer wrong than to do it. To have to endure such a sweet wrong and still remain innocent has got to be the highest form of happiness. [. . .]

Oh, Melchior, girls enjoy themselves like the gods in heaven! A girl protects herself by her very nature. She keeps herself free from bitterness till the last moment. And then, then, all at once, she feels heaven descend upon her like a soft cloud. A girl is afraid of hell even at the moment she sees paradise spread before her. Her emotions are as fresh as water springing from a rock. A girl lifts up a chalice that no earthly being has touched, a flaming, flickering chalice of nectar that she drinks at a single gulp — I think the satisfaction that a man receives at a time like that must be hollow and dull by comparison.

Spring's Awakening

Frank Wedekind

Translated by Carl R. Mueller

Teens

Seriocomic

Moritz Steifel, speaking to his wiser young friend Melchior, is frustrated that he doesn't know the facts of life. He enlists his friend's help.

I see how hens lay eggs, and they say mother carried me under her heart, but what the hell does that mean? I still remember when I was five, I got embarrassed when the Queen of Hearts was turned up, with her dress cut clear down to here. Well, I got over that. But today it's all I can do to talk to a girl without thinking something disgusting. And I swear, Melchior, I don't know what! [. . .]

I've gone through the encyclopedia from A to Z and it's all words, words! Not one explanation! God, and the shame! Why have an encyclopedia that doesn't answer the most obvious question in the world! [. . .]

But you can do me a favor. Write down everything you know, short and clear as you can, and stuff it between my books tomorrow during gym class. I'll take it home without knowing and discover it all at once. And I couldn't keep from reading it if I was dead tired. And, well, if you think it'd help, you could make some drawings in the margins.

Stark Naked

Georges Feydeau
Translated by Charles Marowitz

45+
Comic

Ventroux, a politician with aspirations, tries to convince his wife she should put some clothes on.

You must never forget that you are married to a man with an unlimited political future. How would it sit with the government if they discovered that a Minister of State has a wife who traipses through the house without clothes on? Disastrous, Clarisse, disastrous! And you know, the wonderful thing about this regime is anyone can aspire to become President of the Republic. And if such an honor befell me, well just consider for a moment . . . We'd have to entertain Kings, Queens, Foreign Dignitaries. Would you officiate at such occasions wearing a transparent nightie? [. . .]

Even though Petard Himmelfaahrt is a low-brow, beady-eyed rodent of the first water, you must remember he is a well-respected entrepreneur. His textile mill employs over six hundred workers, which means six hundred votes, Clarisse. You must be sickeningly pleasant to him at all costs, and we must humor him. (*Looking at his watch.*) He'll be here any moment. Go, go get dressed!

Stark Naked

Georges Feydeau

Translated by Charles Marowitz

30s

Comic

Jaival, a self-important reporter, arrives at the house of Monsieur Ventroux, a politician.

(*Entering rapidly and coming straight up to Ventroux, almost nose-to-nose.*) 'sieur Ventroux. I am Romain de Jaival from Le Figaro. I have been sent by my paper to interview you, 'sieur Ventroux. They would like an in-depth piece, with accompanying photos, both amusing and informative and brilliantly composed, and so naturally, they sent me. On political questions mainly . . . Your last few speeches have placed you squarely in the public eye. There is great interest in your ideas, particularly your most recent proposal about birth control among the farm workers, state-sponsored midwives and a special tax on unwed mothers. The thing is I would like to do something fresh and original with this story. I am well known for turning out provocative, and if I do say so myself, astonishing columns. I write daily, as you may know. Perhaps you are familiar with my byline? My father was the first to publish a paper entirely in red ink. You may recall the publication — Les Toutes Rouge. It was suspended when they found the ink was toxic, irremovable and caused septicemia. (*Solemnly.*) Only two or three fatalities, all martyrs to the cause of Journalism. A red hand became a mark of distinction among the press. I wear it myself.

Stark Naked

Georges Feydeau
Translated by Charles Marowitz

40+
Comic

Ventroux, an aspiring politician, apologizes for his wife who wore a transparent nightgown to greet a local dignitary.

I cannot possibly express how mortified I am, 'sieur Himmelfaahr. (*He makes a point of pronouncing it correctly*). The fact is my wife is a fanciful creature who suffers from delusions from time to time. It runs in her family, I fear. Her mother was a certified lunatic — or so her father told me — although he himself was under the impression that he was the reincarnation of Napoleon Bonaparte. [. . .] It is just incredible the things that pop into her head out of her mouth. "Low-brow beady-eyed rodent . . . " is really one of her more extraordinary concoctions. At other times, of course, she behaves quite normally. And you must forgive my wife the manner in which she presented herself. I can assure you she's not in the habit of walking around like that. It is, of course, quite warm today which almost — but not quite — excuses her inexcusable behavior. You felt her hands I'm sure. It is very humid today. Here, just feel mine (*Takes one of Himmelfaahrt's hands between his own.*) Quite damp as you see. (*Himmelfaahrt withdraws his hand and wipes it on his shirt.*) And quite unpleasant.

The Summer People

Maxim Gorky

Translated by Nicholas Saunders and Frank Dwyer

60

Seriocomic

Upon seeing a pretty, young woman, Kolon recalls a happier time.

Oh, there's Basov's wife. What a woman . . . she's a magnet! If only I were about ten years younger . . .

I was [married], yes. And more than once . . . but — some died, some ran away from me . . . and I had children . . . two little girls . . . they died . . . and a little boy . . . he drowned, you know . . . but I've always been lucky with women . . . I got every single one of them right here in Russia, that's where I found them . . . it's not hard to steal away the wife of a Russian! You're terrible husbands . . . Wherever I happened to be, I'd just keep my eyes open — and pretty soon I'd see a woman who needed, you know what I mean, a little attention, and her husband — a cipher in a hat . . . all I had to do was wait under the branches and catch them as they dropped . . . (*He laughs.*) But that's all in the past . . . and now, there's nothing . . . nothing, and no one . . . you see what I mean? . . .

Suppliants

Aeschylus

Translated by Carl R. Mueller

45+

Dramatic

Danaös has fled with his daughters to Argos to protect them from a forced marriage to their cousins. He gives them advice on how to conduct themselves in this new land.

Time is the only test,
the foreigner's only proving-ground,
and we are foreigners here.
We all have sharp tongues to use against
foreigners like us, and it's
easy to let slip a slanderous word;
we must guard against inviting
criticism.
So you must bring no disgrace on me with your
youth that turns men's heads.
Summer fruit is not easily guarded.
Animals, beasts, birds come to
plunder it, as well as men.
What else?
And in matters of love,
Aphroditê spreads her feast in
gardens of desire, and men when
passing the charming beauty of
girls, conquered by the sight,
send out bolts of seductive glances to
enchant them.

Never forget the seas we
fled across to escape this lust of men,
and the pain we suffered in doing so.
Let us not fall to it again.
Let us not shame ourselves, only to
delight our enemies.
A new life awaits, my dears,
and the choice is yours.
To live alone or in company with others,
as the king has offered.
And what's more,
at the city's expense.
That much is easy.
But remember to value
modesty even more than life itself.

Swan Song

Anton Chekhov

Translated by Carol Rocamora

68

Seriocomic

The empty stage of a second-rate provincial theater. An old has-been actor, Svetovidov, describes how a snobbish woman ruined his love for performing.

When I was a young actor, when I was just starting out, in the heat of it all, I remember — a woman in the audience fell in love with me, with my stage persona . . . Elegant, shapely, like a poplar tree, young, innocent, pure, fiery as the summer dawn! A glance from her blue eyes, a flash of her dazzling smile, and night itself could not maintain its darkness. Ocean breakers beat the rocky shores, but waves of her golden curls might have crushed cliffs, melted icebergs, snowdrifts! I remember I stood before her once, just as I stand before you now . . . So lovely was she, lovelier than ever before, and the look that she gave me that day I take with me to my grave . . . Such softness, sweet soulfulness, the velvet of youth, the brilliance of it! Thrilled, ecstatic, I fell on my knees before her, and asked for her hand . . . (*Continues in a hushed voice.*) And she . . . she said: leave the stage! Leave-the-stage! . . . Do you hear me? All well and good to fall in love with an actor, but to marry one — never! I remember, I had a performance that night . . . A crude, clownish role . . . So, I played it, and felt my eyes opening right then and there . . . And then I saw that nothing is sacred about our art, that it's all deceit, delirium, and that I — I am but a slave, an idle plaything, a fool, a buffoon! How well I understood the public then! From that time on I never believed the applause, the bouquets, the wreaths, the rapturous raves . . . Yes, Nikitushka! They applaud me, buy my photograph for a ruble, but I'm an outcast to them — I'm scum, a public prostitute! They seek me out for their vanity, but would they lower themselves to let me marry their sisters, their daughters? . . . No, I don't trust them! (*Sinks down on the stool.*) Not one bit!

The Tempest

William Shakespeare

50–60
Dramatic

Prospero is an exiled duke turned magician. When his dukedom is restored to him, he renounces his magic.

Ye elves of hills, brooks, standing lakes and groves,
And ye that on the sands with printless foot
Do chase the ebbing Neptune and do fly him
When he comes back; you demi-puppets that
By moonshine do the green sour ringlets make,
Whereof the ewe not bites, and you whose pastime
Is to make midnight mushrooms, that rejoice
To hear the solemn curfew; by whose aid,
Weak masters though ye be, I have bedimm'd
The noontide sun, call'd forth the mutinous winds,
And 'twixt the green sea and the azured vault
Set roaring war: to the dread rattling thunder
Have I given fire and rifted Jove's stout oak
With his own bolt; the strong-based promontory
Have I made shake and by the spurs pluck'd up
The pine and cedar: graves at my command
Have waked their sleepers, oped, and let 'em forth
By my so potent art. But this rough magic
I here abjure, and, when I have required
Some heavenly music, which even now I do,
To work mine end upon their senses that
This airy charm is for, I'll break my staff,
Bury it certain fathoms in the earth,
And deeper than did ever plummet sound
I'll drown my book.

The Tenor

Frank Wedekind

Translated by André Tridon

36

Dramatic

When Gerardo, a Wagnerian tenor, is accosted in his hotel room by an obnoxious composer who believes that art is "the highest thing in the world," the seasoned performer wastes no time in setting the young man straight.

Art, my dear man! Let me tell you that art is quite different from what the papers tell us it is. [. . .] We artists are merely a luxury for the use of the *bourgeoisie*. When I stand there on the stage I feel absolutely certain that not one solitary human being in the audience takes the slightest interest in what we, the artist, are doing. If they did, how could they listen to "Die Walküre," for instance? Why, it is an indecent story which could not be mentioned anywhere in polite society. And yet, when I sing Siegmund, the most puritanical mothers bring their fourteen-year-old daughters to hear me. This, you see, is the meaning of whatever you call art. [. . .] Do you know what the artistic wants of the public consist in? To applaud, to send flowers, to have a subject for conversation, tosee and be seen. They pay me half a million, but then I make business for hundreds of cabbies, writers, dressmakers, restaurant keepers. It keeps money circulating; it keeps blood running. It gets girls engaged, spinsters married, wives tempted, old cronies supplied with gossip; a woman loses her pocketbook in the crowd, a fellow becomes insane during the performance. Doctors, lawyers made. . . . (*He coughs.*) And with this I must sing Tristan in Brussels tomorrow night! I tell you all this, not out of vanity but to cure you of your delusions. The measure of a man's worth is the world's opinion of him, not the inner belief which one finally adopts after brooding over it for years. Don't imagine that you are a misunderstood genius. There are no misunderstood geniuses.

Three Hours after Marriage

John Gay

30s

Seriocomic

1777, London. A mere three hours after the wedding ceremony, Fossile intercepts a suggestive note addressed to his new bride and is horrified to learn she may be in love with someone else.

There are now no more Secrets between us. Man and Wife are One.

Madam, Either I mistake the Encouragement I have had, or I am to be happy to-Night. I hope the same Person will compleat her good Offices: I stand to Articles. The Ring is a fine one; and I shall have the Pleasure of putting it on for the first time. This from your impatient, R. P.

In the name of Beelzebub, what is this? *Encouragement! Happy to-Night! same Person! good Offices!* Whom hast thou married, poor Fossile? Couldst thou not divert thyself still with the Spoils of Quarries and Coal-pits, thy Serpents and thy Salamanders, but thou must have a living Monster too! 'Sdeath! what a Jest shall I be to our Club! Is there no Rope among my Curiosities? Shall I turn her out of doors, and proclaim my infamy; or lock her up, and bear my Misfortunes? Lock her up! Impossible. One may shut up Volatile Spirits, pen up the Air, confine Bears, Lyons and Tygers, nay, keep even your Gold: But a Wanton Wife who can keep?

The Three Sisters

Anton Chekhov

Translated by Carol Rocamora

45+

Dramatic

Ivan Romanovich Chebutykin, a failed, alcoholic military doctor, laments.

(*Sullenly.*) To hell with them . . . with all of them . . . They think I'm a doctor, that I can cure all kinds of illnesses, and what do I know? absolutely nothing, I've forgotten everything I ever knew, I remember nothing, absolutely nothing.

To hell with them. Last Wednesday I took care of a woman in Zasyp — she died, and it was my fault, that she died. Yes . . . I might have known something twenty-five years ago, but now, I remember nothing. Nothing. Perhaps I'm not even human, I only seem to have arms, and legs, and a head; perhaps I don't even exist at all, I only seem to walk, and eat, and sleep. (*Weeps.*) Oh, if only I didn't exist at all! (*Stops weeping, sullenly.*) Who the hell knows . . . The other day at the club, they were talking, about Shakespeare, about Voltaire . . . I've never read them, never read any of them, but I seemed to have read them, I gave the impression that I had. And there were others there like me, too. The vulgarity! The vileness of it all! And that woman I murdered on Wednesday, I thought of her . . . I thought of everything, and such an ugly, nasty, foul feeling of loathesomeness descended upon my soul . . . so I started to drink . . .

'Tis Pity She's a Whore

John Ford

20s

Dramatic

Italy. Giovanni, a tragic young man, confesses his forbidden passion for his sister, Annabella .

Lost, I am lost: my fates have doom'd my death.
The more I strive, I love; the more I love,
The less I hope: I see my ruin certain.
What judgment or endeavors could apply
To my incurable and restless wounds
I thoroughly have examin'd, but in vain:
O that it were not in religion sin
To make our love a god and worship it!
I have even wearied heaven with prayers, dried up
The spring of my continual tears, even starv'd
My veins with daily fasts: what wit or art
Could counsel, I have practic'd; but alas,
I find all these but dreams and old men's tales
To fright unsteady youth; I'm still the same.
Or I must speak, or burst; 'tis not, I know,
My lust, but 'tis my fate that leads me on.
Keep fear and low faint-hearted shame with slaves;
I'll tell her that I love her, though my heart
Were rated at the price of that attempt.
O me! She comes.

Two Gentlemen of Verona

William Shakespeare

20s

Comic

Proteus schemes to betray his friend, Valentine, in order to steal his girlfriend.

To leave my Julia, shall I be forsworn;
To love fair Silvia, shall I be forsworn;
To wrong my friend, I shall be much forsworn;
And even that power which gave me first my oath
Provokes me to this threefold perjury;
Love bade me swear and Love bids me forswear.
O sweet-suggesting Love, if thou hast sinned,
Teach me, thy tempted subject, to excuse it!
At first I did adore a twinkling star,
But now I worship a celestial sun.
I will forget that Julia is alive,
Remembering that my love to her is dead;
And Valentine I'll hold an enemy.

Uncle Vanya

Anton Chekhov

Translated by Carol Rocamora

40–50

Dramatic

Marina, the old nurse, is knitting a stocking. Nearby paces Astrov, a doctor who has been called to tend to one of the professor's ailments. Astrov worries that tending the sick has aged him and that his emotions have been deadened.

Third week of Lent, I went to Malitskoe for the epidemic . . . Typhus . . . In the huts, on the floor, wall-to-wall bodies . . . Mud, stench, filth . . . calves on the floor, lying right there, alongside the sick . . . Pigs, too . . . I worked all day long, never sat down, never ate a morsel of food, and no sooner do I get home, not a moment's rest — they bring the switchman over from the railroad yard; I lay him out on the table, you know, for surgery, and he up and dies on me under chloroform. Just like that. Right on the spot. And that's when my feelings come alive again, just when I don't need them . . . and my conscience starts to torment me, as if I'd killed him myself, on purpose . . . I sat down, right then and there, I closed my eyes — just like this, and I thought: those who will live after us, one hundred – two hundred years from now, those for whom we show the way, will they remember us kindly? Will they? No, nanny, they won't!

When We Dead Awaken

Henrik Ibsen

Translated by Rick Davis and Brian Johnston

40s

Dramatic

Rubek, a sculptor, reunites with his model and muse, Irene, after many years. Irene was in love with Rubek, but he could not return her affections.

I was an artist, Irene. First and foremost an artist. And I was sick with desire to create the supreme work of my life. It was to be called "Resurrection Day." To be sculpted in the likeness of a young woman awakening from the sleep of death — Awakening as the noblest, purest, most ideal of women, that's what she was to be. Then I found you. You embodied all I needed. And you agreed so joyfully and willingly. So you then left home and followed me. You were for me a holy creature, to be touched only by thoughts of the purest adoration. I was still a young man at the time, Irene. A superstitious dread possessed me that to touch you, to desire you sensually, would so defile my spirit I would be incapable of giving final form to what I was striving after. And I believe, to this day, there was some truth in that. Thanks and praise to you — I fulfilled my calling. I wanted to shape the pure woman as I envisioned she must appear awakening on Resurrection Day. Not marveling over anything new, or unknown, or unimagined. But filled with a holy joy at discovering herself unchanged — she, a woman of the earth, in this higher, freer, happier region — after the long, dreamless sleep of death. (*Speaking more softly.*) That's how I shaped her. In your image I shaped her, Irene.

When We Dead Awaken

Henrik Ibsen

Translated by Rick Davis and Brian Johnston

40s

Dramatic

Rubek, a sculptor, having been reunited after many years with his past model and muse, breaks off with his live-in girlfriend, Maja.

You really have no clear notion of how an artist's mind works. I live so intensely, Maja. That's how we artists live. For my part I've been through a whole lifetime in the few years we've known each other. And I've come to see it's just not in my nature to find happiness in a life of leisure. That's not how life can be lived for me and my kind. I have to keep active — bringing work after work into being — up to the day I die. (*With difficulty.*) For that reason, I can't go on with you any longer, Maja — No longer with you alone. [. . .]

(*Vehemently.*)Yes, I'm saying I've grown tired of you — intolerably tired and bored and worn-out from living with you. Now you know. (*Controlling himself.*) Those are ugly, brutal words I'm saying. I feel that all too keenly. And you're in no way at fault in this. I'm the one, no one else, who's undergone a transformation — (*Half to himself.*) an awakening to what my own life truly is about.

Women Beware Women

Thomas Middleton

20s

Seriocomic

Leantio is a young man in love with his wife. As he returns home after a day's work, Leantio extols the virtues and joys of matrimony.

How near am I now to a happiness,
That earth exceeds not! not another like it;
The treasures of the deep are not so precious,
As are the conceal'd comforts of a man,
Lockt up in woman's love. I scent the air
Of blessings when I come but near the house;
What a delicious breath marriage sends forth!
The violet-bed's not sweeter. Honest wedlock
Is like a banqueting-house built in a garden,
On which the spring's chaste flowers take delight
To cast their modest odours; when base lust,
With all her powders, paintings, and best pride,
Is but a fair house built by a ditch-side.
When I behold a glorious dangerous strumpet,
Sparkling in beauty and destruction too,
Both at a twinkling, I do liken straight
Her beautifi'd body to a goodly temple
That's built on vaults where carcasses lie rotting,
And so by little and little I shrink back again,
And quench desire with a cool meditation,
And I'm as well methinks. Now for a welcome
Able to draw men's envies upon man:

A kiss now that will hang upon my lip,
As sweet as morning dew upon a rose,
And full as long; after a five days' fast
She'll be so greedy now, and cling about me,
I take care how I shall be rid of her;
And here't begins.

The Women of Trachis

Sophokles
Translated by Carl R. Mueller and
Anna Krajewska-Wieczorek

Teens–20s
Dramatic

To win back her husband's love, Deianeira sent him a charmed robe. But the charm went horribly wrong, and Herakles suffered a terrible fate. Here, their son, Hyllos, describes to his mother how he watched his father die.

Mother, I wish either that you were dead,
Or someone else's mother, not mine!
You've murdered your husband, my father! [. . .]

He was set to begin the great sacrificial slaughter
When Lichas, his herald, appeared bringing from home
Your gift, the fatal robe.
He put it on,
As you had instructed, and began the sacrifice. [. . .]

But then,
Pain in spasmed waves bit into his bones,
And then the venom, as if from some deadly viper,
Began to devour him. [. . .]

Everyone there raised a cry of horror
At the sight, and no one dared
Approach the raging man, who, in his pain,
Dashed himself to the earth, then, screaming in agony,
Flung himself into the air, till the rocks resounded

From Lokris to the cliffs of Euboia.
But when he could no longer move,
Exhausted with throwing himself to the ground,
Lying there groaning and cursing,
Cursing your vileness!
Only then, did his eyes, wild in their sockets,
See me weeping in the crowd.
He called to me: "Son! Come closer! Don't run from me in my agony!
Don't let me die here."
[. . .]
These are the things you've done, Mother.
And I pray that avenging Justice and the Furies
Hound you down and punish you!

The World Well Lost

John Dryden

40s

Dramatic

On the last day of his life, Mark Antony, general of Rome, enjoys a dark and melancholy fantasy of his death.

Lie there, thou shadow of an emperor;
The place thou pressest on thy mother earth
Is all thy empire now: now it contains thee;
Some few days hence, and then 'twill be too large,
When thou'rt contracted in thy narrow urn,
Shrunk to a few cold ashes; then Octavia
(For Cleopatra will not live to see it),
Octavia then will have thee all her own,
And bear thee in her widowed hand to Cæsar;
Cæsar will weep, the crocodile will weep,
To see his rival of the universe
Lie still and peaceful there. I'll think no more on't.
Give me some music; look that it be sad:
I'll soothe my melancholy, till I swell,
And burst myself with sighing. — (*Soft music.*)

RIGHTS AND PERMISSIONS

Every effort has been made to locate the proper holder for each excerpt published in this anthology. Any discrepancies or exclusions are unintentional.

Note that for all books published by Smith and Kraus, inquiries should be addressed to Smith and Kraus Publishers, P.O. Box 127, Lyme, NH 03768 or editor@smithandkraus.com.

Agamemnon by Aeschylus, translated by Carl R. Mueller, as published in *Aeschylus, Complete Plays*, volume I. Reprinted by permission of Smith and Kraus Publishers, Inc. © 2002.

Aias by Sophokles, translated by Carl R. Mueller and Anna Krajewska-Wieczorekk, as published in *Sophokles: The Complete Plays*. Reprinted by permission of Smith and Kraus Publishers, Inc. © 2000.

Alkestis by Euripides, translated by Carl R. Mueller, as published in *Euripides: The Complete Plays*, volume I. Reprinted by permission of Smith and Kraus Publishers, Inc. © 2005.

Andromache by Euripides, translated by Carl R. Mueller, as published in *Euripides: The Complete Plays*, volume II. Reprinted by permission of Smith and Kraus Publishers, Inc. © 2005.

Antigone by Sophokles, translated by Carl R. Mueller and Anna Krajewska-Wieczorekk, as published in *Sophokles: The Complete Plays*. Reprinted by permission of Smith and Kraus Publishers, Inc. © 2000.

Arms and the Man by George Bernard Shaw. © 1930 by George Bernard Shaw. Reprinted by permission of the Society of Authors. For further information, contact the Society of Authors, 84 Drayton Gardens, London, England, SW10 9SB.

Back from the Country by Carlo Goldoni, translated by Robert Cornthwaite, as published in *Villeggiatura: A Trilogy*. Reprinted by permission of Smith and Kraus Publishers, Inc. © 1994.

The Bakkhai by Euripides, translated by Carl R. Mueller, as published in *Euripides: The Complete Plays*, volume IV. Reprinted by permission of Smith and Kraus Publishers, Inc. © 2005.

The Bear by Anton Chekhov, translated by Carol Rocamora, as published in *Chekhov: "The Vaudevilles" and Other Short Works*. Reprinted by permission of Smith and Kraus Publishers, Inc. © 1998.

Changes of the Heart (The Double Inconstancy) by Pierre de Marivaux, translated by Stephen Wadsworth, as published in *Marivaux: Three Plays*. Reprinted by permission of Smith and Kraus Publishers, Inc. © 1999.

The Cherry Orchard by Anton Chekhov, translated by Carol Rocamora, as published in *Chekhov: Four Plays*. Reprinted by permission of Smith and Kraus Publishers, Inc. © 1996.

Children of Herakles by Euripides, translated by Carl R. Mueller, as published in *Euripides: The Complete Plays*, volume I. Reprinted by permission of Smith and Kraus Publishers, Inc. © 2005.

Cyrano de Bergerac by Edmond Rostand, English version translated by Charles Marowitz, as published in *Cyrano de Bergerac*. Reprinted by permission of Smith and Kraus Publishers, Inc. © 1995.

Danton's Death by Georg Büchner, translated by Henry J. Schmidt. © 1986. Reprinted by permission of The Continuum Publishing Company. For further information contact The Continuum Publishing Company, 370 Lexington Avenue, New York, NY 10017.

A Doll House by Henrik Ibsen, translated by Rick Davis and Brian Johnston, as published in *Ibsen, Volume I: Four Major Plays*. Reprinted by permission of Smith and Kraus Publishers, Inc. © 1995.

Elektra by Sophokles, translated by Carl R. Mueller and Anna Krajewska-Wieczorekk, as published in *Sophokles: The Complete Plays*. Reprinted by permission of Smith and Kraus Publishers, Inc. © 2000.

An Enemy of the People by Henrik Ibsen, translated by Rick Davis and Brian Johnston, as published in *Ibsen, Volume I: Four Major Plays*. Reprinted by permission of Smith and Kraus Publishers, Inc. © 1995.

Eumenides by Aeschylus, translated by Carl R. Mueller, as published in *Aeschylus: The Complete Plays*, volume I. Reprinted by permission of Smith and Kraus Publishers, Inc. © 2002.

The Father by August Strindberg, translated by Carl R. Mueller, as published in *August Strindberg: Five Major Plays*. Reprinted by permission of Smith and Kraus Publishers, Inc. © 2000.

Faust by Johann Wolfgang von Goethe, translated by Carl R. Mueller, as published in *Faust: Part One*. Reprinted by permission of Smith and Kraus Publishers, Inc. © 2004.

Ghosts by Henrik Ibsen, translated by Rick Davis and Brian Johnston, as published in *Ibsen, Volume I: Four Major Plays*. Reprinted by permission of Smith and Kraus Publishers, Inc. © 1995.

The Green Cockatoo by Arthur Schnitzler, translated by Carl R. Mueller, as published in *Arthur Schnitzler: Four Major Plays*. Reprinted by permission of Smith and Kraus Publishers, Inc. © 1999.

Hippolytus by Euripides, translated by Carl R. Mueller, as published *Euripides: The Complete Plays*, volume I. Reprinted by permission of Smith and Kraus Publishers, Inc. © 2005.

Ivanov by Anton Chekhov, translated by Carol Rocamora, as published in *Chekhov: The Early Plays*. Reprinted by permission of Smith and Kraus Publishers, Inc. © 1999.

John Gabriel Borkman by Henrik Ibsen, translated by Rick Davis and Brian Johnston, as published in *Ibsen, Volume III: Four Plays*. Reprinted by permission of Smith and Kraus Publishers, Inc. © 1998.

Judith by Friedrich Hebbel, translated by Marion W. Sonnenfeld. Originally published by Associated University Presses, Inc. Reprinted by permission of Associated University Presses, Inc. © 1974. For further information contact Associated University Presses, 440 Forsgate Drive, Cranbury, NJ 08512.

La Ronde by Arthur Schnitzler, translated by Carl R. Mueller as published in *Arthur Schnitzler: Four Major Plays*. Reprinted by permission of Smith and Kraus Publishers, Inc. © 1999.

Leonce and Lena by Georg Büchner, translated by Henry J. Schmidt. Reprinted by permission of The Continuum Publishing Company. © 1986. For further information contact The Continuum Publishing Company, 370 Lexington Avenue, New York, NY 10017.

The Libation Bearers by Aeschylus, translated by Carl R. Mueller, as published in *Aeschylus: The Complete Plays*, volume I. Reprinted by permission of Smith and Kraus Publishers, Inc. © 2002.

Medeia by Euripides, translated by Carl R. Mueller, as published in *Euripides: The Complete Plays*, volume I. Reprinted by permission of Smith and Kraus Publishers, Inc. © 2005.

Oedipus Tyrannos by Sophokles, translated by Carl R. Mueller and Anna Krajewska-Wieczorekk, as published in *Sophokles: The Complete Plays*. Reprinted by permission of Smith and Kraus Publishers, Inc. © 2000.

On the Harmful Effects of Tobacco by Anton Chekhov, translated by Carol Rocamora, as published in *Chekhov: "The Vaudevilles" and Other Short Works*. Reprinted by permission of Smith and Kraus Publishers, Inc. © 1998.

Oresteia by Aeschylus, translated by Carl R. Mueller, as published in *Aeschylus: The Complete Plays*, volume I. Reprinted by permission of Smith and Kraus Publishers, Inc. © 2002.

Orestes by Euripides, translated by Carl R. Mueller, as published in *Euripides: The Complete Plays*, volume IV. Reprinted by permission of Smith and Kraus Publishers, Inc. © 2005.

Persians by Aeschylus, translated by Carl R. Mueller, as published in *Aeschylus: The Complete Plays*, volume II. Reprinted by permission of Smith and Kraus Publishers, Inc. © 2002.

Phoenician Women by Euripides, translated by Carl R. Mueller, as published in *Euripides: The Complete Plays*, volume IV. Reprinted by permission of Smith and Kraus Publishers, Inc. © 2005.

The Prince of Homburg by Heinrich von Kleist, translated by Carl R Mueller, as published in *Heinrich von Kleist: Three Major Plays*. Reprinted by permission of Smith and Kraus Publishers, Inc. @ 2000.

Prometheus Bound by Aeschylus, translated by Carl R. Mueller, as published by *Aeschylus: Complete Plays*, volume II. Reprinted by permission of Smith and Kraus Publishers, Inc. © 2002.

The Seagull by Anton Chekhov, translated by Carol Rocamora, as published in *Chekhov: Four Plays*. Reprinted by permission of Smith and Kraus Publishers, Inc. © 1996.

Seven Against Thebes by Aeschylus, translated by Carl R. Mueller, as published in *Aeschylus: Complete Plays*, volume II. Reprinted by permission of Smith and Kraus Publishers, Inc. © 2002.

Spring's Awakening by Frank Wedekind, translated by Carl R. Mueller, as published in *Frank Wedekind: Four Major Plays*. Reprinted by permission of Smith and Kraus Publishers, Inc. © 2000.

The Stronger by August Strindberg, translated by Carl R. Mueller, as published in *August Strindberg: Five Major Plays*. Reprinted by permission of Smith and Kraus Publishers, Inc. © 2000.

Suppliants by Aeschylus, translated by Carl R. Mueller, as published in *Aeschylus: The Complete Plays*, volume II. Reprinted by permission of Smith and Kraus Publishers, Inc. © 2002.

Swan Song by Anton Chekhov, translated by Carol Rocamora, as published in *Chekhov: "The Vaudevilles" and Other Short Works*. Reprinted by permission of Smith and Kraus Publishers, Inc. © 1998.

The Three Sisters by Anton Chekhov, translated by Carol Rocamora, as published in *Chekhov: Four Plays*. Reprinted by permission of Smith and Kraus Publishers, Inc. © 1996.

Trojan Women by Euripides, translated by Carl R. Mueller, as published in *Euripides: The Complete Plays*, volume III. Reprinted by permission of Smith and Kraus Publishers, Inc. © 2005.

Uncle Vanya by Anton Chekhov, translated by Carol Rocamora, as published in *Chekhov: Four Plays*. Reprinted by permission of Smith and Kraus Publishers, Inc. © 1996.

When We Dead Awaken by Henrik Ibsen, translated by Rick Davis and Brian Johnston, as published in *Ibsen, Volume III: Four Plays*. Reprinted by permission of Smith and Kraus Publishers, Inc. © 1998.

The Wild Duck by Henrik Ibsen, translated by Rick Davis and Brian Johnston, as published in *Ibsen, Volume II: Four Plays*. Reprinted by permission of Smith and Kraus Publishers, Inc. © 1998.

The Women of Trachis by Sophokles, translated by Carl R. Mueller and Anna Krajewska-Wieczorekk, as published in *Sophokles: The Complete Plays*. Reprinted by permission of Smith and Kraus Publishers, Inc. © 2000.

Irene Ziegler Aston is an actor and writer living in Richmond, Virginia. Her play, *Rules of the Lake,* won the Mary Roberts Rinehart award. Irene narrated the award-winning documentary film, *In the Face of Evil: Ronald Reagan's War in Word and Deed.* She is completing a novel.

John Capecci is a communications consultant and writer based in Minneapolis. He holds a Ph.D. in Performance Studies and has taught communication performance methods for over fifteen years.